CW00409418

Published by Kando Consulting
1st Edition printed September 2014

Copyright © Kando Consulting Ltd 2014

All rights reserved. No part of this publication may be reproduced, stored in a retrieval system, or transmitted in any form or by any means, electronic, mechanical, photocopying, recording or otherwise without the prior written permission of the Publisher. This book may not be lent, resold, hired out or otherwise disposed of by way of trade in any form of binding or cover other than that in which it is published, without the prior consent of the Publisher.

Acknowledgements to:
Austin Foenander
Philip Gore B.Sc(Hons), PGCE, MA

CONTENTS

INTRODUCTION

KANDO comes from the Japanese word 'kano', meaning an inspired state of mind. And that's just what we aim to deliver with the KANDO Emotional Intelligence Programme – an inspired way of looking at life, understanding your emotions and using that knowledge wisely.

The idea of emotional intelligence is not new. For years, psychologists and psychoanalysts have realised its importance and sought to define it.

In this book we'll look at some of the greatest exponents of emotional intelligence and their theories that shaped the way we view our lives, giving practical frameworks for understanding our emotional development.

You'll read about Erik Erikson – famous for coming up with the term 'identity crisis' – who spent much of his life as one of the world's leading psychologists/psychoanalysts researching and developing a model of psychosocial development that serves as a guide to personal development throughout life. It identifies steps and stages and the lessons in life that, if learned, mark our development as a person. This development is a journey, an idea that was embraced by Abraham Maslow, who explained that everyone has basic needs, and only if they are met can we truly become autonomous and empathetic individuals. Maslow's theory of motivation of humans 'The Hierarchy of Needs' is still regarded as one of the most important pieces of work in this field – more about that later.

Experts in the fields of human development and learning recognise that it is not merely the acquisition of knowledge or facts in isolation that matters: true learning involves both information and emotional intelligence. If the two are not in synthesis, the process can be stifled and impinge on our relationships throughout childhood, adulthood, at work and with our family and friends.

You'll also read about 'pedagogy' or 'androgogy' used in relation to learning and Emotional Intelligence. The theory has been in existence since the Greeks coined the name for the most effective way to learn, experience and excel at performing in a way to achieve a desired outcome.

In practice, it means simply leading your child to an activity as opposed to telling them what to do and making them do it without you. Instead, do it with them and teach what they are doing as you go along. Explain what they are doing and why. Then make sure you ask them to teach you what they have just learned from you. This reinforces their understanding, gives the child a feeling of achievement and pride, and ensures you know they have understood.

It is the two-way learning processes that teaches you better how to engage your child and teaches them how to do what you have learned at least 50% quicker than it took you to learn it. This is what underpins the KANDO Emotional Intelligence Programme

Pedagogy is a valid way of teaching throughout the education system – to university level and beyond, and EMOTIONAL INTELLIGENCE remains vital. Every year, thousands of young people get degrees. They have undoubtedly learned many facts but how many of them have informed opinions about everyday life and the challenges facing society? Do they think about challenges such as feeding the world's population or the legal system in Somalia? Do they know how to listen to a lonely old person and how to recognise and act when their friends are sad?

Development is not about knowledge per se (facts as facts alone) but understanding, how to generalise concepts and apply them creatively. If we are careless, this aspect becomes an afterthought to education rather than a key component. To ameliorate this, the answer is simple – start early. Not just p's and q's but EQs!

It's been shown that people with high EQ communicate better with other people in their lives. They're better at recognising and understanding others' feelings.

In short, people with high EQ are empathetic opposed to apathetic.

To achieve that for yourself, read the book then take action. See how you feel when you reach out and unlock your emotional intelligence and teach your children to do the same. It's already in there – you just need to recognise and use it.

THE KANDO EQ / IQ BALANCE

KANDO is having an inspired state of mind. It's a balance of the knowledge we have and the tools to use it effectively, in any circumstances.

We all know examples of very intelligent people – with a high IQ – who don't succeed in life or love while those of modest IQ succeed. Why is that? It's because they may be conventionally 'clever' but their EQ is not so hot – and without that it's hard to do your best at work or in personal relationships.

How well you do in your life and career is determined by both your IQ and your EQ. IQ alone is not enough; EQ also matters. In fact, psychologists generally agree that among the ingredients for success, IQ counts for roughly 10% (at best 25%); the rest depends on everything else – including EQ.

THE TUG-OF-WAR BETWEEN IQ AND EQ

The readily recognisable IQ (intelligence quotient) is not enough on its own but, combined with good EQ, there's the best basis for success.

What do you think is more important to success: (a) brain power or (b) intuition? Which does a successful person need more of: (a) book learning or (b) people skills? Studies have shown the b's have it.

A Harvard study of its graduates revealed there is little or no correlation between IQ indicators (such as entrance exam scores) and subsequent career success.

As the global economy expands and the world shrinks, people with the ability to understand other people, and then interact with them so that each is able to achieve their goals, will be the success stories of the future. People will realise that a high EQ is the key to a thriving career.

If all decisions are in the end emotional, should we spend some of our time understanding ourselves better and this in- built gift of Emotional Intelligence? The seeds are planted in us all; when we choose to grow them is up to you.

> *'In the end, all decisions are emotional. We lay out the factors but the final decision is emotional.'*
>
> EDWARD DE BONO

EMOTIONAL INTELLIGENCE (EI)

EASY TO LEARN, A LIFETIME TO MASTER

This book focuses on emotional intelligence and our understanding of this important area of the human lifecycle development. It shows how EI helps us develop as individuals, and gives you an insight on EI as a framework for us to use, helping us integrate it into our lives and grow effectively to achieve physical health, mental well-being and successful outcomes throughout our lives.

Knowledge alone is not enough; we need to recognise and understand our emotions and those of others so our emotional intelligence can help us be at our most effective.

WHAT IS EI AND HOW IS IT MEASURED?

Emotional Intelligence is basically the ability to understand other people, what motivates them and how to work co-operatively with them. The five major categories of EI are self-awareness, self-regulation, motivation, empathy and social skills.

To improve emotional intelligence, first you need to assess how well developed it is. Emotional quotient is a notional measurement of this intelligence that gauges a person's ability to identify, assess and manage emotions – both their own and others'. Scientific research demonstrates the importance of EI in developing emotional stability, inter-personal skills, creativity, leadership skills and stress management.

For generations, family and friends have passed on the majority of our emotional intelligence knowledge. As our technology has advanced a rift has begun to form in these connections. Neurology research has proved that this disconnect will only continue to spread, 'If you don't use it, you will lose it.' Have you ever met someone chronologically aged 40, but emotionally aged nine? What if the hunter gatherers never passed each other their knowledge of how to catch food effectively? This is a good example of how members of our society can fall through the cracks if we let this happen.

WHY IS EI IMPORTANT?

For most people, emotional intelligence, measured as EQ, is more important than intelligence (IQ) in attaining success in their lives and careers. As individuals, our success and the success of the enterprise today, depend on our ability to read other people's signals and react appropriately to them.

Therefore, each one of us must develop the mature emotional intelligence skills required to better understand, empathise and negotiate with other people - particularly as the economy has become more global. Otherwise, success will elude us in our lives and careers.

'Wisdom comes from the seeds of life; it would be a shame to wait till we reach 60 to grow them'.

DOES EI MATTER?

There are lots of ways at looking at the complex world we live in today – lots of ways to interpret how we act and why. It seems that we've never had a keener interest in the psychological perspectives of our world. Some try to understand life from a religious perspective, others from a scientific viewpoint, and some people and groups develop their own understanding based on individual preferences and beliefs.

In this book we start at the beginning of life. We recognise that parents – female and male – have the same in-built instincts to protect and educate their children. We're not interested here in a scientific review of genealogy or why people are born with certain characteristics or temperaments – what we are interested in is what we can all do next to get the best out of ourselves and our children to meet the challenges of an ever evolving world that we live in.

We refer to some of the world's experts in the field to provide a framework, together with some tools that can be used for understanding. This isn't a 'one size fits all' system or solution: what you learn here can be applied to you and your family, as individuals, to meet your needs and help you all be the best you can. The answer in the end is the same: it's all about YOU.

WHAT CAN EI DO FOR YOU?

Would you like to have done your PHD and when someone offers you double what you're earning forget to let them tell you what it is they are wanting of you?

I mean just telling them about your knowledge is great but there are loads of PhD's given out every year, Isn't it what you can do with your knowledge and how this might relate to a value in society as important as the knowledge itself?

With EQ you can do both without EQ you can only explain how cleaver you are in the context of what you have learned.

With EI you can do both; without EI you can only explain how clever you are in the context of what you have learned.

HOW DO INDIVIDUALS BENEFIT?

Would a person like to know about knowledge alone or know a lot about themselves, their own and others' emotions and how to relate their knowledge to an audience?

For instance, it's said that he who can talk is only telling himself and others what they already know, but those who can listen to others and can relate what they know to others have EI in their lives.

Can you just talk about what you know or can you listen and relate it to others?

THE 5 CATEGORIES OF EI

Your EQ is the level of your ability to understand other people, what motivates them and how to work co-operatively with them. Emotional Intelligence researchers say these abilities are observed in five major categories.

1. SELF-AWARENESS

The ability to recognise an emotion as it 'happens' is the key to your EI. Developing self-awareness requires tuning in to your true feelings. If you evaluate your emotions, you can manage them. The major elements of self-awareness are:

- Emotional awareness: your ability to recognise your own emotions and their effects.

- Self-confidence: sureness about your self-worth and capabilities.

2 .SELF-REGULATION

You often have little control over when you experience emotions. You can, however, have some say in how long an emotion will last by using different techniques to alleviate negative emotions such as anger, anxiety or depression. A few of these techniques include recasting a situation in a more positive light, taking a long walk and meditation or prayer. Self-regulation involves:

- Self-control: managing disruptive impulses.

- Trustworthiness: maintaining standards of honesty and integrity.

- Conscientiousness: taking responsibility for your own performance.

- Adaptability: handling change with flexibility.

- Innovation: being open to new ideas.

3. MOTIVATION

To motivate yourself for any achievement requires clear goals and a positive attitude. Although you may have a predisposition to either a positive or a negative attitude, you can, with effort and practice, learn to think more positively. If you catch negative thoughts as they occur, you can reframe them in more positive terms - which will help you achieve your goals. Motivation is made up of:

- Achievement drive: your constant striving to improve or to meet a standard of excellence.

- Commitment: aligning with the goals of the group or organisation.

- Initiative: readying yourself to act on opportunities.

- Optimism: pursuing goals persistently despite obstacles and setbacks.

4. EMPATHY

Being able to recognise how people can help you succeed at work and in your personal life. The more skilful you are at discerning the feelings behind others' signals the better you can control the signals you send them. An empathetic person excels at:

- Service orientation: anticipating, recognising and meeting clients' needs.

- Developing others: sensing what others need to progress and bolstering their abilities.

- Leveraging diversity: cultivating opportunities through diverse people.

- Political awareness: reading a group's emotional currents and power relationships.

- Understanding others: discerning the feelings behind the needs and wants of others.

5. SOCIAL SKILLS

The development of good interpersonal skills is tantamount to success in your life and career. In today's always-connected world, everyone has immediate access to technical knowledge. 'People skills' are even more important now because you must possess a high EQ to better understand, empathise and negotiate with people from all over the world in a global economy. Among the most useful skills are:

- <u>Influence:</u> wielding effective persuasion tactics.

- <u>Communication:</u> sending clear messages.

- <u>Leadership:</u> inspiring and guiding groups and people.

- <u>Change catalyst:</u> initiating or managing change.

- <u>Conflict management:</u> understanding, negotiating and resolving disagreements.

- <u>Building bonds:</u> nurturing instrumental relationships.

- <u>Collaboration and co-operation:</u> working with others toward shared goals.

- <u>Team capabilities:</u> creating group synergy in pursuing collective goals.

A BRIEF HISTORY OF EI

'All learning has an emotional base'

PLATO

The twentieth century saw a surge in the number and breadth of psychological theories striving to understand how and why we interact with others around us in the way that we do. This often led to simplistic models; a variety of one size fits all explanations of how we function mentally. Most people have heard of the concept of IQ (intelligence quotient), but many scientists see it as a just one of the inadequate models that as George Miller wrote, did not explain 'man as man.'

Over the years we've evolved a more complex understanding of ourselves. The following highlights some significant stages in this:

- Edward Thorndike describes the concept of 'social intelligence' as the ability to get along with other people (1930s).

- David Wechsler suggests that affective components of intelligence may be essential to success in life (1940s).

- Humanistic psychologists such as Abraham Maslow describe how people can build emotional strength (1950s).

- Howard Gardner publishes *The Shattered Mind*, which introduces the concept of multiple intelligences (1975).

- Wayne Payne introduces the term emotional intelligence in his doctoral dissertation entitled *A study of emotion: Developing emotional intelligence* (1985).

- Keith Beasley uses the term 'emotional quotient' in an article published in *Mensa Magazine* (1987). It has been suggested that this is the first published use of the term, though Reuven-Bar claims to have used the term in an unpublished version of his graduate thesis.

- Psychologists Peter Salovey and John Mayer publish their landmark article *Emotional Intelligence* in the journal *Imagination, Cognition and Personality* (1990).

- Daniel Goleman popularises the term and developed related concepts in his influential book *Emotional Intelligence: Why it can matter more than IQ* (1995).

- Goleman in *Working with Emotional Intelligence* (1998) explores the function of EI in the workplace. According to Goleman EI is the largest single predictor of success in the workplace.

- Payne's thesis centres on the idea that society's historical repression of emotion is the source of widespread problems such as addiction, depression, illness, religious conflict, violence and war.

- Salovey and Mayer have been the leading researchers on Emotional Intelligence since 1990. In their article emotional intelligence is defined as 'the subset of social intelligence that involves the ability to monitor one's own and others' feelings and emotions, to discriminate among them and to use this information to guide one's thinking and actions.'

- Goleman and others develop the concept of a testable EQ (Emotional Intelligence quotient). As a counterpart to IQ, an EQ test focuses more on the individual's capacity to deal effectively with others. This evaluates traits and abilities such as self-awareness and empathy, which are sometimes referred to as soft skills.

- Goleman describes Emotional Intelligence as 'managing feelings so that they are expressed appropriately and effectively, enabling people to work together smoothly toward their common goals.' He says there are four major skills that comprise Emotional Intelligence:

  - Self awareness

  - Self management

  - Social awareness

  - Relationship management.

SUMMARISING THE BENEFITS OF EI

Psychology Today describes EQ as 'the ability to identify your own emotions and the emotions of others.'

EI includes three primary skills, which hold for both children and adults:

- <u>Using emotions effectively.</u> Emotionally intelligent people use their emotions to help them think and problem solve in school and work.

- <u>Identify emotions properly.</u> Emotionally intelligent people are able to accurately identify the feelings of themselves and others.

- <u>Regulating emotions skilfully.</u> EI people can harness their own emotions and also use their empathetic responses to others in helpful ways.

Identifying feelings and learning to empathise does not come naturally to everyone. Regardless of the ease with which people learn EI, the skill is extremely important throughout life. People who are emotionally appropriate are more pleasant to be around than those who are not.

According to <u>Six Seconds</u> (a California based organisation supporting Emotional Intelligence in schools, businesses and families around the world) some of the specific benefits of Emotional Intelligence for children include:

- <u>Academic success.</u> Children with higher EQ perform better in schools as a whole than their peers with lower scores.

- <u>Academic retention.</u> Children with higher EQ are less likely to drop out of high school or college than children with lower EQ scores.

- <u>Increased pro-social behaviour.</u> Children with higher EQ tend to be more adept at navigating relationships, co-operating and responding compassionately and appropriately with friends, at home and at school.

To summarise, the learnable, measurable skills of Emotional Intelligence predict increased achievement, stronger relationships and healthier decisions. The research is clear: social and emotional factors are the drivers or limiters of learning. When children, and of course the adults who support them, are engaged, curious, sure and thriving then they achieve.

Emotional intelligence is the capacity to blend thinking and feeling (and understand the differences and which is which!) to make optimal decisions. This is the key to having a successful relationship with yourself and others. The model of Emotional Intelligence in action begins with three important pursuits: to become more aware (noticing what you do), more intentional (doing what you mean) and more purposeful (doing it for a reason).

Know yourself is to clearly see what you feel and do. Emotions are a form of data, and these competencies allow you to accurately collect that information. Know yourself gives you the what – when you know yourself you know your strengths and challenges, you know what you are doing, what you want, what to change.

Choose yourself is doing what you mean to do. Instead of reacting on 'autopilot' these competencies allow you to proactively respond. Choose yourself provides the how – it shows you how to take action, how to influence yourself and others, how to 'operationalise' these concepts.

Give yourself is doing for a reason. These competencies help you put your vision and mission into action so you lead on purpose and with full integrity. Give yourself delivers the why – when you give yourself you are clear and full of energy so you stay focused on why to respond in a certain way, why to move in a new direction, and why others should come on board.

THE SIX SECOND MODEL OF EMOTIONAL INTELLIGENCE

Know yourself
Clearly seeing what you feel and do. Emotions are data, and these competencies allow you to accurately collect that information.

Choose yourself
Doing what you mean to do. Instead of reacting 'on autopilot,' these competencies allow you to proactively respond.

Give Yourself

<u>Doing it for a reason</u>. These competencies help you put your vision and mission into action so you lead on purpose and with full integrity.

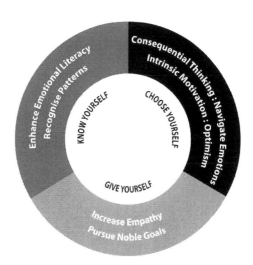

The what, how and why

Know Yourself gives you the 'what' – when you Know Yourself, you know your strengths and challenges, you know what you are doing, what you want, and what to change.

Choose Yourself provides the 'how' – it shows you how to take action, how to influence yourself and others, how to 'operationalise' these concepts.

Give Yourself delivers the 'why' – when you Give Yourself you are clear and full of energy so you stay focused on why to respond a certain way, why to move in a new direction, and why others should come on board.

You'll notice we present the model in a CIRCLE – it's not a list, it's a process!

In the Six Seconds model at the core of Emotional Intelligence will help you be more emotionally intelligent and smarter with your feelings. Using the model will help you more accurately recognise emotions in yourself and others. This data will help you make decisions and find solutions to the 'life puzzles' we all face.

Pursuit	Competency	Definition
KNOW YOURSELF	Enhance emotional literacy	Accurately identifying and interpreting both simple and compound feelings
	Recognise patterns	Acknowledging frequently recurring reactions and behaviours
CHOOSE YOURSELF	Apply consequential thinking	Evaluating the costs and benefits of your choices
	Navigate emotions	Assessing, harnessing and transforming emotions as a strategic resource
	Engage intrinsic motivation	Gaining energy from personal values and commitments v. being driven by external forces
	Exercise optimism	Taking a proactive perspective of hope and possibility
GIVE YOURSELF	Increase empathy	Recognizing and appropriately responding to others' emotions
	Pursue noble goals	Connecting your daily choices with your overarching sense of purpose

THE KANDO EI FRAMEWORK

Here we look at four key frameworks in theory and language that will help put KANDO EQ in context and give us a model that best applies to our own experience as we develop EI.

We'll cover the development of adult EI in a future book; for now we're concentrating on children up to the age of 12, and how we can help them develop their EI.

In this section we'll examine the significance of the following four key frameworks as they relate to children and Emotional Intelligence:

- Erikson's eight stages of Human Lifecycle Development

- Maslow's 'Hierarchy of Needs'

- Pedagogy

- Lev Vagotsky

To give us a framework of understanding we'll start with an overview of Eric Erikson's 'psychosocial' development theory. You may find other similar frameworks that draw the same conclusions, in which case, use the one that you are most comfortable with. This is a framework for understanding and not the answer. To find your own personal solution you need to take action to realise the benefits of your in-built EI.

ERIKSON'S LIFE CYCLE MODEL

Erikson's model of psychosocial development, first published in 1950 and continually developed for another fifty years, is a very significant, highly regarded and meaningful concept. It says that life is a series of lessons and challenges that help us to grow. His theory helps us understand how we continue to learn and grow, and is equally relevant for child development and adults.

THE 8 AGES OF MAN			
Erikson's psychosocial crisis stages (syntonic v dystonic)	Life stage	Basic virtue and second named strength (potential positive outcomes from each crisis)	Maladaption / malignancy (potential negative outcome - one or the other - from unhelpful experience during each crisis)
1. Trust v mistrust	infant	Hope and drive	Sensory distortion / withdrawal
2. Autonomy v shame & doubt	toddler	Willpower and self-control	Impulsivity / compulsion
3. Initiative v guilt	preschool	Purpose and direction	Ruthlessness / inhibition
4. Industry v inferiority	schoolchild	Competence and method	Narrow virtuosity / inertia
5. Identity v role confusion	adolescent	Fidelity and devotion	Fanaticism / repudiation
6. Intimacy v isolation	young adult	Love and affiliation	Promiscuity / exclusivity
7. Generativity v stagnation	mid-adult	Care and production	Overextension / rejectivity
8. Integrity v despair	late adult	Wisdom and renunciation	Presumption / disdain

Of course we can't hope to do more than give a brief overview here, so for more information we'd recommend that you read Erikson's books; he was an award-winning writer and he conveyed his theory in a very readable and interesting way. It's fascinating to see how his ideas develop over time, perhaps aided by his own journey through the 'psychosocial crisis' stages model that underpinned his work.

Erikson's model has been described as a biopsychosocial or bio-psycho-social theory (bio refers to biological, which in this context means life); Erikson's human development cycle or life cycle, and other variations. All refer to the same eight stages psychosocial theory, it being Erikson's most distinct work and remarkable model.

Erikson called it his 'psychosocial' theory, from the words psychological (mind) and social (relationships).

He believed that his psychosocial principle occurs in everyone and is genetically inevitable in shaping human development.

He also referred to his theory as 'epigenesis' and the 'epigenetic principle', which signified the concept's relevance to evolution (past and future) and genetics.

Erikson said that in the word 'epigenesis', 'ep' can mean 'above' in space as well as 'before' in time, and with 'genesis' represents the space-time nature of all development...' from *Vital Involvement in Old Age*, 1989

So in Erikson's theory, epigenetic doesn't refer to individual genetic make-up and its influence on individual development. Erikson, like Freud, was largely concerned with how personality and behaviour is influenced after birth - not before birth - and especially during childhood. In the 'nature v nurture' (genes v experience) debate, Erikson was firmly focused on nurture and experience.

THE EIGHT STAGES OF PSYCHOSOCIAL DEVELOPMENT

Like other seminal concepts, Erikson's model is simple and elegant, yet very sophisticated. The theory is a basis for broad or complex discussion and analysis of personality and behaviour, and also for understanding and for facilitating personal development - of self and others.

The main elements of the theory covered in this explanation are:

- Erikson theory overview
- The Freudian stages of psychosexual development
- Erikson's 'psychosocial crises' (or crisis stages)
- Basic virtues (basic strengths)
- Maladaptions and Malignancies Erikson terminology

Please note that we use the terms 'positive' and 'negative' in the summary to identify the first or second factors in each crisis (e.g. trust = positive; mistrust = negative) however no crisis factor (disposition or emotional force - whatever you choose to call them - descriptions are quite tricky as even Erikson found) is actually wholly positive or wholly negative. Healthy personality development is based on a sensible balance between 'positive' and 'negative' dispositions at each crisis stage. Erikson didn't use the words positive and negative in this sense. He tended to use 'syntonic' and 'dystonic' to differentiate between the two sides of each crisis. Those words won't mean much to the lay reader so we use the more recognisable 'positive' and 'negative' terms, despite them being potentially misleading. You should also qualify your use of these terms if using them in relation to the crisis stages.

ERIKSON'S PSYCHOSOCIAL THEORY - SUMMARY DIAGRAM

Here's a broad introduction to the main features of Erikson's model. Various people have produced different interpretations like this grid below. Erikson produced a few charts of his own too, from different perspectives, but he seems never to have produced a fully definitive matrix. To aid explanation and use of his theory he produced several perspectives in grid format, some of which he advocated be used as worksheets. He viewed his concept as an evolving work in progress. This summary attempts to show the main points of the Erikson psychosocial crisis theory of human development. More detail follows this overview.

Erikson's psychosocial crisis stages (syntonic v dystonic)	Freudian psycho-sexual stages	Life stage / relationships / issues	Basic virtue and second named strength (potential positive outcomes from each crisis)	Maladaptation / malignancy (potential negative outcome - one or the other - from unhelpful experience during each crisis)
1. Trust v mistrust	Oral	infant / mother / feeding and being comforted, teething, sleeping	Hope and drive	Sensory distortion / withdrawal
2. Autonomy v shame & doubt	Anal	toddler / parents / bodily functions, toilet training, muscular control, walking	Willpower and self-control	Impulsivity / compulsion
3. Initiative v guilt	Phallic	preschool / family / exploration and discovery, adventure and play	Purpose and direction	Ruthlessness / inhibition
4. Industry v inferiority	Latency	schoolchild / school, teachers, friends, neighbourhood / achievement and accomplishment	Competence and method	Narrow virtuosity / inertia
5. Identity v role confusion	Puberty and genitality	adolescent / peers, groups, influences / resolving identity and direction, becoming a grown-up	Fidelity and Devotion	Fanaticism / repudiation
6. Intimacy v isolation	(Genitality)	young adult / lovers, friends, work connections / intimate relationships, work and social life	Love and affiliation	Promiscuity / exclusivity
7. Generativity v stagnation	n/a	mid-adult / children, community / 'giving back', helping, contributing	Care and production	Overextension / rejectivity
8. Integrity v despair	n/a	late adult / society, the world, life / meaning and purpose, life achievements	Wisdom and renunciation	Presumption / disdain

This chart attempts to capture and present concisely the major elements of Erikson's theory, drawn from various Erikson books, diagrams and other references, including *Childhood and Society* (1950); *Identity and the Life Cycle* (1959); *The Life Cycle Completed: A Review* (1982, revised 1996 by Joan Erikson); and *Vital Involvement in Old Age* (1989). Erikson later suggested psychosexual stages 7 and 8, but they are not typically part of Freud's scheme which extended only to puberty/genitality. See Freud's psychosexual stages below.

ERIK ERIKSON'S PSYCHOSOCIAL THEORY OVERVIEW

Erikson's psychosocial theory is widely and highly regarded. As with any concept there are critics, but generally Erikson's theory is considered fundamentally significant. Erikson was a psychoanalyst and also a humanitarian, so his theory is useful far beyond psychoanalysis - it's useful for any application involving personal awareness and development - of oneself or others.

There is a strong, but not essential, Freudian element in Erikson's work and model. Fans of Freud will find the influence useful. People who disagree with Freud, and especially his psychosexual theory, can ignore the Freudian aspect and still find Erikson's ideas useful. Erikson's theory stands alone and does not depend on Freud for its robustness and relevance.

Aside from Freudian psychoanalysis, Erikson developed his theory mainly from his extensive practical field research, initially with Native American communities, and then also from his clinical therapy work attached to leading mental health centres and universities. He actively pioneered psychoanalytical development from the late 1940s until the 1990s.

Crucially, Erikson's concept incorporated cultural and social aspects into existing Freud's biological and sexually oriented theory.

Erikson was able to do this because of his strong interest and compassion for people, especially young people, and also because his research was carried out among human societies far removed from the more inward-looking world of the psychoanalyst's couch, which was essentially Freud's approach.

This helps Erikson's eight stages theory to be a tremendously powerful model: it is very accessible and obviously relevant to modern life, from several different perspectives, for understanding and explaining how personality and behaviour develops. The relevance means that Erikson's theory is useful for teaching, parenting, self-awareness, managing and coaching, dealing with conflict, and generally for understanding self and others.

Both Erikson and his wife Joan, who collaborated as psychoanalysts and writers, were passionately interested in childhood development, and its effects on adult society. Erikson's work is as relevant today as when he first outlined his original theory, in fact given the modern pressures on society, family and relationships - and the quest for personal development and fulfilment - his ideas are probably more relevant now than ever.

Put simply, Erikson's psychosocial theory says that people experience eight 'psychosocial crisis stages' in their lives. And each of those eight crisis stages significantly affects every individual's development and personality. Joan Erikson described a 'ninth' stage after Erik's death, but the eight stage model is most commonly referenced and is regarded as the standard. (Joan Erikson's work on the 'ninth stage' appears in her 1996 revisions to *The Life Cycle Completed: A Review*.)

Erikson's theory refers to 'psychosocial crisis' (or the plural, psychosocial crises). This term is an extension of Sigmund Freud's use of the word 'crisis', which represents internal emotional conflict. You might also describe this sort of crisis as an internal struggle or challenge that a person must negotiate and deal with in order to grow and develop.

Erikson's 'psychosocial' term is derived from the two source words - namely psychological (or the root, 'psycho' relating to the mind, brain, personality, etc) and social (external relationships and environment), both at the heart of Erikson's theory. Occasionally you'll see the term extended to biopsychosocial, in which bio refers to life, as in biological.

Each stage involves a crisis of two opposing emotional forces. A helpful term used by Erikson for these opposing forces is 'contrary dispositions'. Each crisis stage relates to a corresponding life stage and its inherent challenges. Erikson used the words 'syntonic' for the first-listed 'positive' disposition in each crisis (e.g. trust) and 'dystonic' for the second-listed 'negative' disposition (e.g. mistrust). To signify the opposing or conflicting relationship between each pair of forces or dispositions, Erikson connected them with the word 'versus', which he abbreviated to 'v'. (Versus is Latin, meaning turned towards or against.) The actual definitions of the syntonic and dystonic words are mainly irrelevant unless you have a passion for the detailed history of Erikson's ideas.

Successfully passing through each crisis involves 'achieving' a <u>healthy ratio or balance</u> between the two opposing dispositions that represent each crisis. For example a healthy balance at crisis stage one (trust v mistrust) might be described as experiencing and growing through the crisis 'trust' (of people, life and one's future development) and also experiencing and growing a suitable capacity for 'mistrust' where appropriate, so as not to be hopelessly unrealistic or gullible, nor to be mistrustful of everything. A child might experience and growing through stage two (autonomy v shame & doubt) to be essentially 'autonomous' (to be one's own person and not a mindless or quivering follower) but to have sufficient capacity for 'shame and doubt', so as to be free-thinking and independent, while also being ethical, considerate and responsible.

Erikson called these successful balanced outcomes 'Basic Virtues' or 'Basic Strengths'. He identified one particular word to represent the fundamental strength gained at each stage, which appear commonly in Erikson's diagrams and written theory, and other explanations of his work. Erikson also identified a second supporting 'strength' word at each stage, which along with the basic virtue, emphasised the main healthy outcome at each stage, and helped convey simple meaning in summaries and charts. Examples of basic virtues and supporting strengths words are 'hope and drive' (from stage one, trust v mistrust) and 'willpower and self-control' (from stage two, autonomy v shame & doubt). It's very useful however to gain a more detailed understanding of the meaning behind these words, because although Erikson's choice these words is very clever, and the words are very symbolic, using just one or two words alone is not adequate for truly conveying the depth of the theory, and particularly the emotional and behavioural strengths that arise from healthy progression through each crisis.

Erikson was sparing in his use of the word 'achieve' in the context of successful outcomes, because it implied gaining something clear-cut and permanent. Psychosocial development is not clear-cut and is not irreversible: any previous crisis can effectively revisit anyone, albeit in a different guise, with successful or unsuccessful results. This perhaps helps explain how 'high achievers' can fall from grace, and how 'hopeless failures' can ultimately achieve great things. No-one should become complacent, and there is hope for us all.

Later in his life Erikson was keen to warn against interpreting his theory as an 'achievement scale', in which the crisis stages represent single safe achievement or target of the extreme 'positive' option, secured once and for ever. Erikson said (in *Identity and the Life Cycle*):

> '...What the child acquires at a given stage is a certain ratio between the positive and negative, which if the balance is toward the positive, will help him to meet later crises with a better chance for unimpaired total development...'

> ERIK ERIKSON

He continued (using rather complicated language, so we'll paraphrase) that at no stage can a 'goodness' be achieved that is impervious to new conflicts, and that to believe so is dangerous and inept.

The crisis stages are not sharply defined steps. Elements tend to overlap and mingle from one stage to the next and to the preceding stages. It's a broad framework and concept, not a mathematical formula that replicates precisely across all people and situations.

Erikson was keen to point out that the transition between stages is 'overlapping'. Crisis stages connect with each other like inter-laced fingers, not like a series of neatly stacked boxes. People don't suddenly wake up one morning and be in a new life stage. Changes don't happen in regimented clear-cut steps: they are graduated, mixed-together and organic. In this respect the 'feel' of the model is similar to other flexible human development frameworks (for example, Elisabeth Kübler-Ross's *Grief Cycle*, and Maslow's *Hierarchy of Needs*).

Where a person passes <u>unsuccessfully</u> through a psychosocial crisis stage they develop a tendency towards one or other of the opposing forces (either to the syntonic or the dystonic, in Erikson's language), which then becomes a behavioural tendency, or even a mental problem. In crude terms we might call this 'baggage' or a 'hang-up'. Those words wouldn't be used in a serious analysis, but they do illustrate that Erikson's ideas are very much related to real life and the way ordinary people think and wonder about things.

Erikson called an extreme tendency towards the syntonic (first disposition) a 'maladapation', and he identified specific words to represent the maladapation at each stage. He called an extreme tendency towards the dystonic (second disposition) a 'malignancy', and again he identified specific words to represent the malignancy at each stage.

Erikson emphasised the significance of and 'mutuality' and 'generativity' in his theory. The terms are linked. Mutuality reflects the effect of generations on each other, especially among families, and particularly between parents and children and grandchildren. Everyone potentially affects everyone else's experiences as they pass through the different crisis stages. Generativity, actually a named disposition within one of the crisis stages (generativity v stagnation, stage seven), reflects the significant relationship between adults and the best interests of children - one's own children, and in a way everyone else's children - the next generation, and all following generations.

Generations affect each other. A parent obviously affects the child's psychosocial development, but in turn the parent's psychosocial development is affected by their experience of dealing with the child and the pressures produced, and it's the same for grandparents. Again, this helps explain why as parents (or teachers or siblings or grandparents) we can often struggle to deal well with a young person when it's as much as we can do to deal with our own emotional challenges.

In some ways, the development actually peaks at stage seven, since stage eight is more about taking stock and coming to terms with how one has made use of life, and ideally preparing to leave it feeling at peace. The perspective of giving and making a positive difference for future generations echoes Erikson's humanitarian philosophy, and it's this perhaps more than anything else that enabled him to develop such a powerful concept.

ERIKSON'S PSYCHOSOCIAL THEORY IN MORE DETAIL

Freud's influence on Erikson's theory

Erikson's psychosocial theory of the 'eight stages of human development' drew from and extended the ideas of Sigmund Freud and Freud's daughter Anna Freud, and particularly the four (or five, depending on interpretation) Freudian stages of development, known as Freud's psychosexual stages or Freud's sexual theory. These concepts are fundamental to Freudian thinking and are outlined below in basic terms relating to Erikson's psychosocial stages.

Freud's concepts, while influential on Erikson, are not however fundamental to Erikson's theory, which stands up perfectly well in its own right.

It is not necessary therefore to understand or agree with Freud's ideas in order to appreciate and use Erikson's theory. If you naturally relate to Freud's ideas fine, otherwise leave them to one side.

Part of Erikson's appeal is that he built on Freud's ideas in a socially meaningful and accessible way - and in a way that did not wholly rely on adherence to fundamental Freudian thinking. Some of Freud's theories by their nature tend attract a lot of attention and criticism - sex, breasts, genitals, and bodily functions generally do - and if you are distracted or put off by these references then ignore them, because they are not crucial for understanding and using Erikson's model.

Freud's psychosexual stages - overview

Age guide is a broad approximation, hence the overlaps. The stages happen in the sequence shown in the following table, but not to a fixed timetable.

Freudian psychosexual stages - overview	Erikson's psychosocial crisis stages	Age guide
1. Oral Stage - feeding, crying, teething, biting, thumb-sucking, weaning - the mouth and the breast are the centre of all experience. The infant's actual experiences and attachments to mum (or maternal equivalent) through this stage have a fundamental effect on the unconscious mind and thereby on deeply rooted feelings, which along with the next two stages affect all sorts of behaviours and (sexually powered) drives and aims - Freud's 'libido' - and preferences in later life.	1. Trust v mistrust	0-1½ yrs, baby, birth to walking
2. Anal Stage - it's a lot to do with pooh - 'holding on' or 'letting go' - the pleasure and control. Is it dirty? Is it okay? Bodily expulsions are the centre of the world, and the pivot around which early character is formed. Am I pleasing my mum and dad? Are they making me feel good or bad about my bottom? Am I okay or naughty? Again the young child's actual experiences through this stage have a deep effect on the unconscious and behaviours and preferences in later life.	2. Autonomy v shame and doubt	1-3 yrs, toddler, toilet training
3. Phallic Stage - phallic is not restricted to boys. This stage is focused on resolving reproductive issues. This is a sort of dry run before the real game starts in adolescence. Where do babies come from? Can I have a baby? Why has dad got a willy and I've not? Why have I got a willy and mum hasn't? Why do they tell me off for touching my bits and pieces down there? (Boys) I'm going to marry mum (and maybe kill dad). (Girls) I'm in love with my dad. Oedipus complex, Electra complex, penis envy, castration anxiety, etc. 'If you touch yourself down there it'll fall off/heal up.' Inevitably once more, experiences in this stage have a profound effect on feelings and behaviour and libido in later life. If you want to know more about all this we recommend you read about Freud, not Erikson, but remember that understanding Freud's psychosexual theory is not required for understanding and using Erikson's concepts.	3. Initiative v guilt	3-6 yrs, pre-school, nursery
4. Latency Stage - sexual dormancy or repression. The focus is on learning, skills, schoolwork. This is actually not a psychosexual stage because normally nothing formative happens sexually. Experiences, fears and conditioning from the previous stages have already shaped many of the child's feelings and attitudes and these will re-surface in the next stage.	4. Industry v inferiority	5-12 yrs, early school

Freudian psychosexual stages - overview	Erikson's psychosocial crisis stages	Age guide
5. Genital stage - puberty in other words. Glandular, hormonal, and physical changes in the adolescent child's body cause a resurgence of sexual thoughts, feelings and behaviours. Boys start treating their mothers like woman-servants and challenge their fathers (Freud's 'Oedipus'). Girls flirt with their fathers and argue with their mums (Freud/Jung's 'Electra'). All become highly agitated if away from a mirror for more than half an hour (Freud's Narcissus or Narcissism). Dating and fondling quickly push schoolwork and sports (and anything else encouraged by parents and figures of authority) into second place. Basically everyone is in turmoil and it's mostly to do with growing up, which entails more sexual undercurrents than parents would ever believe, even though these same parents went through exactly the same struggles themselves just a few years before. It's a wonder anyone ever makes it to adulthood, but of course they do, and mostly it's all perfectly normal. This is the final Freudian psychosexual stage. Erikson's model, which from the start offers a different and more socially oriented perspective, continues through to old age, and re-interprets Freudian sexual theory into the adult life stages equating to Erikson's crisis stages. This incorporation of Freudian sexual stages into the adult crisis stages is not especially significant.	5. Identity v role confusion	11-18 yrs, puberty, teens earlier for girls
Arguably no direct equivalent Freudian stage, although as from Identity and the Life Cycle (1969) Erikson clearly separated Puberty and Genitality (Freud's Genital stage), and related each respectively to identity v role confusion, and intimacy v isolation.	6. Intimacy v isolation	18-40, courting, early parenthood
No direct equivalent Freudian stage, although Erikson later interpreted this as being a psychosexual stage of 'procreativity'.	7.Generativity v stagnation	30-65, middle age, parenting
Again no direct equivalent Freudian stage. Erikson later called this the psychosexual stage of 'Generalization of Sensual Modes'.	8. Integrity v despair	50+, old age, grandparents

This is a brief overview of Freud's sexual theory and where it equates to Erikson's crisis stages and is not meant to be a serious detailed analysis of Freud's psychosexual ideas.

Erikson's eight psychosocial crisis stages

Here's a more detailed interpretation of Erikson's psychosocial crisis stages.

Remember age range is just a very rough guide, especially through the later levels when parenthood timing and influences vary. Hence the overlap between the age ranges in the interpretation below. Interpretations of age range vary among writers and academics. Erikson intentionally did not stipulate clear fixed age stages, and it's impossible for anyone to do so.

Below is a reminder of the crisis stages, using the crisis terminology of the original 1950 model. The 'Life Stage' names were suggested in later writings by Erikson and did not appear so clearly in the 1950 model. Age range and other descriptions are general interpretations and were not shown specifically like this by Erikson. Erikson's main terminology changes are explained below.

Crisis stages are driven by physical and sexual growth, which then prompts the life issues which create the crises. The crises are therefore not driven by age precisely. Erikson never showed precise ages, and I prefer to state wider age ranges than many other common interpretations. The final three (adult) stages happen at particularly variable ages.

It's worth noting also that these days there's a lot more 'life' and complexity in the final (old age) stage than when the eight stages were originally outlined, which no doubt fuelled Joan Erikson's ideas on a 'ninth stage' after Erik's death.

* Other interpretations of the Adolescence stage commonly suggest stage 5 begins around 12 years of age. This is reasonable for most boys, but given that Erikson and Freud cite the onset of puberty as the start of this stage, stage 5 can begin for girls as early as age nine.

Psychosocial Crisis Stage	Life Stage	Age range, other descriptions
1. Trust v mistrust	Infancy	0-1½ yrs, baby, birth to walking
2. Autonomy v shame and doubt	Early childhood	1-3 yrs, toddler, toilet training
3. Initiative v guilt	Play age	3-6 yrs, pre-school, nursery
4. Industry v inferiority	School age	5-12 yrs, early school
5. Identity v role confusion	Adolescence	9-18 yrs, puberty, teens*
6. Intimacy v isolation	Young adult	18-40, courting, early parenthood
7. Generativity v stagnation	Adulthood	30-65, middle age, parenting
8. Integrity v despair	Mature age	50+, old age, grandparent

Erikson's psychosocial theory essentially states that each person experiences eight 'psychosocial crises' (internal conflicts linked to life's key stages) which help to define his or her growth and personality.

People experience these 'psychosocial crisis' stages in a fixed sequence, but timings vary according to people and circumstances.

This is why the stages and the model are represented primarily by the names of the crises or emotional conflicts themselves (such as trust v mistrust) rather than strict age or life stage definitions. Age and life stages do feature in the model, but as related rather than pivotal factors, and age ranges are increasingly variable as the stages unfold.

Each of the eight 'psychosocial crises' is characterised by a conflict between two opposing positions or attitudes (or dispositions or emotional forces). Erikson never really settled on a firm recognisable description for the two components of each crisis, although in later works the first disposition is formally referred to as the 'Adaptive Strength'. He also used the terms 'syntonic' and 'dystonic' for respectively the first and second dispositions in each crisis, but not surprisingly these esoteric words never featured strongly in interpretations of Erikson's terminology, and their usual meanings are not very helpful in understanding what Erikson meant in this context.

The difficulty in 'labelling' the first and second dispositions in each crisis is a reflection that neither is actually wholly good or bad, or wholly positive or negative. The first disposition is certainly the preferable tendency, but an ideal outcome is achieved only when it is counter-balanced with a degree of the second disposition.

Successful development through each crisis is requires a balance and ratio between the two dispositions, not total adoption of the apparent 'positive' disposition, which if happens can produce almost as much difficulty as a strong or undiluted tendency towards the second 'negative' disposition.

Some of the crisis stages are easier to understand than others. Each stage contains far more meaning than can be conveyed in just two or three words. Crisis stage one is 'Trust versus Mistrust', which is easier to understand than some of the others. Stage four 'Industry versus Inferiority' is a little trickier. You could say instead 'usefulness versus uselessness' in more modern common language. Erikson later refined 'Industry' to 'Industriousness', which probably conveys a fuller meaning.

Successful passage through each stage is dependent on <u>striking the right balance between the conflicting extremes</u> rather than entirely focusing on (or being guided towards) the 'ideal' or 'preferable' extreme in each crisis. In this respect Erikson's theory goes a long way to explaining why too much of anything is not helpful for developing a well-balanced personality.

A well-balanced positive experience during each stage develops a corresponding '<u>basic virtue</u>' (or 'basic strength - a helpful personality development), each of which enables a range of other related emotional and psychological strengths. For example passing successfully through the Industry versus Inferiority crisis (stage four, between 6-12 years of age for most people) produces the 'basic psychosocial virtue' of 'competence' (plus related strengths such as 'method', skills, techniques, ability to work with processes and collaborations, etc).

Where passage through a crisis stage is less successful (in other words not well-balanced, or worse still, psychologically damaging) then to a varying extent the personality acquires an unhelpful emotional or psychological tendency, which corresponds to one of the two opposite extremes of the crisis concerned.

Neglect and failure at any stage is problematical, but so is too much emphasis on the apparent 'good' extreme.

For example unsuccessful experiences during the Industry versus Inferiority crisis would produce a tendency towards being overly focused on learning and work, or the opposite tendency towards uselessness and apathy. Describing these unhelpful outcomes, Erikson later introduced the terms 'maladaptation' (overly adopting 'positive' extreme) and 'malignancy' (adopting the 'negative' extreme). In the most extreme cases the tendency can amount to serious mental problems.

Erikson's psychosocial crisis stages - meanings and interpretations

Erikson used particular words to represent each psychosocial crisis. As ever, single words can be misleading and rarely convey much meaning. Here is more explanation of what lies behind these terms.

Erikson reinforced these crisis explanations with a perspective called 'psychosocial modalities', which in the earlier stages reflect Freudian theory, and which are paraphrased below. They are not crucial to the model, but they do provide a useful additional viewpoint.

'Psychosocial crisis' / 'psychosocial modality'	Meaning and interpretation
1. Trust v mistrust 'To get' 'To give in return' (To receive and to give in return. Trust is reciprocal - maybe 'karma' even.)	The infant will develop a healthy balance between trust and mistrust if fed and cared for and not over-indulged or over-protected. Abuse or neglect or cruelty will destroy trust and foster mistrust. Mistrust increases a person's resistance to risk-exposure and exploration. 'Once bitten twice shy' is an apt analogy. On the other hand, if the infant is insulated from all and any feelings of surprise and normality, or unfailingly indulged, this will create a false sense of trust amounting to sensory distortion, in other words a failure to appreciate reality. Infants who grow up to trust are more able to hope and have faith that 'things will generally be okay'. This crisis stage incorporates Freud's psychosexual Oral stage, in which the infant's crucial relationships and experiences are defined by oral matters, notably feeding and relationship with mum. Erikson later shortened 'Basic trust v basic mistrust' to simply Trust v Mistrust, especially in tables and headings.

'Psychosocial crisis' / 'psychosocial modality'	Meaning and interpretation
2. Autonomy v shame & doubt 'To hold on' 'To let go' (To direct behaviour outward or be retentive. Of course very Freudian...)	Autonomy means self-reliance. This is independence of thought, and a basic confidence to think and act for oneself. Shame and doubt mean what they say, and obviously inhibit self-expression and developing one's own ideas, opinions and sense of self. Toilet and potty training is a significant part of this crisis, as in Freud's psychosexual Anal stage, where parental reactions, encouragement and patience play an important role in shaping the young child's experience and successful progression through this period. The significance of parental reaction is not limited to bottoms and pooh - it concerns all aspects of toddler exploration and discovery while small children struggle to find their feet - almost literally - as little people in their own right. The 'terrible twos' and 'toddler tantrums' are a couple of obvious analogies which represent these internal struggles and parental battles. The parental balancing act is a challenging one, especially since parents themselves are having to deal with their own particular psychosocial crisis, and of course deal with the influence of their own emotional triggers which were conditioned when they themselves passed through earlier formative crisis stages. What are the odds that whenever a parent berates a child, 'That's dirty...' it will be an echo from their own past experience at this very stage?
3. Initiative v guilt 'To make (= going after)' 'To 'make like' (= playing)' (To make and complete things, and to make things together. To pursue ideas, plans)	Initiative is the capability to devise actions or projects, and a confidence and belief that it is okay to do so, even with a risk of failure or making mistakes. Guilt means what it says, and in this context is the feeling that it is wrong or inappropriate to instigate something of one's own design. Guilt results from being admonished or believing that something is wrong or likely to attract disapproval. Initiative flourishes when adventure and game-playing is encouraged, irrespective of how daft and silly it seems to the grown-up in charge. Suppressing adventure and experimentation, or preventing young children doing things for themselves because of time, mess or a bit of risk will inhibit the development of confidence to initiate, replacing it instead with an unhelpful fear of being wrong or unapproved. The fear of being admonished or accused of being stupid becomes a part of the personality. 'If I don't initiate or stick my neck out I'll be safe...' (from feeling guilty and bad). Parents, carers and older siblings have a challenge to get the balance right between giving young children enough space and encouragement so as to foster a sense of purpose and confidence, but to protect against danger, and also to enable a sensible exposure to trail and error, and to the consequences of mistakes, without which an irresponsible or reckless tendency can develop.

'Psychosocial crisis' / 'psychosocial modality'	Meaning and interpretation
	This crisis stage correlates with Freud's psychosexual Phallic stage, characterised by a perfectly natural interest in genitals, where babies come from, and as Freud asserted, an attachment to the opposite sex parent, and the murky mysteries of the Oedipus Complex, Penis Envy and Castration Anxiety, about which further explanation and understanding is not critical to appreciating Erikson's theory.
	What's more essential is to recognise that children of this age are not wicked or bad or naughty, they are exploring and experimenting very naturally in pursuit of learning, development and confidence. The parental/carer responsibility is therefore to provide children with sufficiently safe situations allowing trial and error, so that supervisory limiting or criticizing or reprimanding can be avoided, and freedoms for adventure and discovery - and consequential development of confidence and initiative - are maximized.
4. Industry v inferiority 'To make (= going after)' 'To 'make like' and complete things, and to make things together' (To initiate projects or ideas, and to collaborate and cooperate with others to produce something.)	Industry here refers to purposeful or meaningful activity. It's the development of competence and skills, and a confidence to use a 'method', and is a crucial aspect of school years experience. Erikson described this stage as a sort of 'entrance to life'. This correlates with Freud's psychosexual Latency stage, when sexual motives and concerns are largely repressed while the young person concentrates on work and skills development. A child who experiences the satisfaction of achievement - of anything positive - will move towards successful negotiation of this crisis stage. A child who experiences failure at school tasks and work, or worse still who is denied the opportunity to discover and develop their own capabilities and strengths and unique potential, quite naturally is prone to feeling inferior and useless. Engaging with others and using tools or technology are also important aspects of this stage. It is like a rehearsal for being productive and being valued at work in later life. Inferiority is feeling useless; unable to contribute, unable to cooperate or work in a team to create something, with the low self-esteem that accompanies such feelings.
	Erikson knew this over fifty years ago. How is it that the people in charge of children's education still fail to realise this? Develop the child from within. Help them to find and excel at what they are naturally good at, and then they will achieve the sense of purpose and industry on which everything else can then be built.

'Psychosocial crisis' / 'psychosocial modality'	Meaning and interpretation
5. Identity v role confusion 'To be oneself (or not to be)' 'To share being oneself' (To be yourself and to share this with others. Affirmation or otherwise of how you see yourself.)	Identity means essentially how a person sees themselves in relation to their world. It's a sense of self or individuality in the context of life and what lies ahead. Role Confusion is the negative perspective - an absence of identity - meaning that the person cannot see clearly or at all who they are and how they can relate positively with their environment. This stage coincides with puberty or adolescence, and the reawakening of the sexual urge whose dormancy typically characterises the previous stage. Young people struggle to belong and to be accepted and affirmed, and yet also to become individuals. In itself this is a big dilemma, aside from all the other distractions and confusions experienced at this life stage. Erikson later replaced the term 'Role confusion' with 'Identity diffusion'. In essence they mean the same.
6. Intimacy v isolation 'To lose and find oneself in another' (Reciprocal love for and with another person.)	Intimacy means the process of achieving relationships with family and marital or mating partner(s). Erikson explained this stage also in terms of sexual mutuality - the giving and receiving of physical and emotional connection, support, love, comfort, trust, and all the other elements that we would typically associate with healthy adult relationships conducive to mating and child-rearing. There is a strong reciprocal feature in the intimacy experienced during this stage - giving and receiving - especially between sexual or marital partners. Isolation conversely means being and feeling excluded from the usual life experiences of dating and mating and mutually loving relationships. This logically is characterised by feelings of loneliness, alienation, social withdrawal or non-participation. Erikson also later correlated this stage with the Freudian Genitality sexual stage, which illustrates the difficulty in equating Freudian psychosexual theory precisely to Erikson's model. There is a correlation but it is not an exact fit.
7. Generativity v stagnation 'To make be' 'To take care of' (Unconditional, non-reciprocating care of one's children, or other altruistic outlets)	Generativity derives from the word generation, as in parents and children, and specifically the unconditional giving that characterises positive parental love and care for their offspring. Erikson acknowledged that this stage also extends to other productive activities - work and creativity for example - but given his focus on childhood development, and probably the influence of Freudian theory, Erikson's analysis of this stage was strongly oriented towards parenting. Generativity potentially extends beyond one's own children, and also to all future generations, which gives the model ultimately a very modern globally responsible perspective.

'Psychosocial crisis' / 'psychosocial modality'	Meaning and interpretation
	Positive outcomes from this crisis stage depend on contributing positively and unconditionally. We might also see this as an end of self-interest. Having children is not a prerequisite for Generativity, just as being a parent is no guarantee that Generativity will be achieved. Caring for children is the common Generativity scenario, but success at this stage actually depends on giving and caring - putting something back into life, to the best of one's capabilities.
	Stagnation is an extension of intimacy which turns inward in the form of self-interest and self-absorption. It's the disposition that represents feelings of selfishness, self-indulgence, greed, lack of interest in young people and future generations, and the wider world. Erikson later used the term 'Self-Absorption' instead of 'Stagnation' and then settled, later, with the original 'Stagnation'.
	Stagnation and/or Self-Absorption result from not having an outlet or opportunity for contributing to the good or growth of children and others, and potentially to the wider world.
8. Integrity v despair 'To be, through having been To face not being' (To be peaceful and satisfied with one's life and efforts, and to be accepting that life will end.)	This is a review and closing stage. The previous stage is actually a culmination of one's achievement and contribution to descendents, and potentially future generations everywhere.
	Later Erikson dropped the word 'Ego' (from 'Ego Integrity') and extended the whole term to 'Integrity v Disgust and despair'. He also continued to use the shorter form 'Integrity v despair'.
	Integrity means feeling at peace with oneself and the world. No regrets or recriminations. The linking between the stages is perhaps clearer here than anywhere: people are more likely to look back on their lives positively and happily if they have left the world a better place than they found it - in whatever way, to whatever extent. There lies Integrity and acceptance.
	Despair and/or 'Disgust' (i.e., rejective denial, or 'sour grapes' feeling towards what life might have been) represent the opposite disposition: feelings of wasted opportunities, regrets, wishing to be able to turn back the clock and have a second chance.
	This stage is a powerful lens through which to view one's life - even before old age is reached.
	Erikson had a profound interest in humanity and society's well-being in general. This crisis stage highlights the issue very meaningfully.
	Happily these days for many people it's often possible to put something back, even in the depths of despair. When this happens people are effectively rebuilding wreckage from the previous stage, which is fine.

Erikson's basic psychosocial virtues or strengths (positive outcomes)

The chart below identifies the 'basic psychosocial virtues' - and related strengths - which result from successfully passing through each crisis. Erikson described success as a 'favourable ratio' (between the two extremes) at each crisis stage.

A basic virtue is not the result of simply achieving the positive extreme of each crisis. Basic virtue is attained by a helpful balance, albeit towards the 'positive', between the two extremes. Helpfully balanced experience leads to positive growth.

Chief life stage issues and relationships are also re-stated as a reminder as to when things happen.

'Basic psychological virtue' and 'basic virtue' (same thing), are Erikson's terminology.

Erikson identified one basic virtue, plus another virtue (described below a 'secondary virtue') for each stage. At times he referred to 'basic virtues' as 'basic strengths'.

A bit confusing, but the main point is that based on what observed for each stage he identified one clear basic virtue and one secondary virtue. From this he was able to (and we can too - he encouraged people to do so) extrapolate other related strengths.

Bear in mind also that the first disposition in each crisis is also inevitably a related strength that comes from successfully experiencing each stage.

Erikson recognised this by later referring to the first disposition (e.g., Trust, Autonomy, etc) as an 'Adaptive Strength'.

BASIC VIRTUES AND OTHER STRENGTHS		
Crisis including adaptive strength	Basic virtue & secondary virtue (and related strengths)	Life stage / relationships / issues
1. Trust v mistrust	Hope & drive (faith, inner calm, grounding, basic feeling that everything will be okay - enabling exposure to risk, a trust in life and self and others, inner resolve and strength in the face of uncertainty and risk)	infant / mother / feeding and being comforted, teething, sleeping
2. Autonomy v shame & doubt	Willpower & self-control (self-determination, self-belief, self-reliance, confidence in self to decide things, having a voice, being one's own person, persistence, self-discipline, independence of thought, responsibility, judgement)	toddler / parents / bodily functions, toilet training, muscular control, walking
3. Initiative v guilt	Purpose & direction (sense of purpose, decision-making, working with and leading others, initiating projects and ideas, courage to instigate, ability to define personal direction and aims and goals, able to take initiative and appropriate risks)	preschool / family / exploration and discovery, adventure and play
4. Industry v inferiority	Competence & method (making things, producing results, applying skills and processes productively, feeling valued and capable of contributing, ability to apply method and process in pursuit of ideas or objectives, confidence to seek and respond to challenge and learning, active busy productive outlook)	schoolchild / school, teachers, friends, neighbourhood / achievement and accomplishment
5. Identity v role confusion	Fidelity & devotion (self-confidence and self-esteem necessary to freely associate with people and ideas based on merit, loyalty, social and interpersonal integrity, discretion, personal standards and dignity, pride and personal identity, seeing useful personal role(s) and purpose(s) in life)	adolescent / peers, groups, influences / resolving identity and direction, becoming a grown-up
6. Intimacy v isolation	Love & affiliation (capacity to give and receive love - emotionally and physically, connectivity with others, socially and inter-personally comfortable, ability to form honest reciprocating relationships and friendships, capacity to bond and commit with others for mutual satisfaction - for work and personal life, reciprocity - give and take - towards good)	young adult / lovers, friends, work connections / intimate relationships, work and social life

BASIC VIRTUES AND OTHER STRENGTHS		
Crisis including adaptive strength	Basic virtue & secondary virtue (and related strengths)	Life stage / relationships / issues
7. Generativity v atagnation	Care & production (giving unconditionally in support of children and/or for others, community, society and the wider world where possible and applicable, altruism, contributing for the greater good, making a positive difference, building a good legacy, helping others through their own crisis stages	mid-adult / children, community / 'giving back', helping, contributing
8. Integrity v despair	Wisdom & renunciation (calmness, tolerance, appropriate emotional detachment - non-projection, no regrets, peace of mind, non-judgemental, spiritual or universal reconciliation, acceptance of inevitably departing)	late adult / society, the world, life / meaning and purpose, life achievements, acceptance

Erikson and Maslow correlations?

You'll see correlations between Erikson's psychosocial model, and parts of Maslow's Hierarchy of Needs. Their perspectives are different but the two systems 'overlap' in places and it's interesting to use them together. The table below includes Erikson's 'Related Elements of Social Order' for comparison.

Life stage / relationships / issues	Crisis	Virtue outcomes	Erikson's 'related elements of social order'	Maslow Hierarchy of Needs stage - primary correlation
Infant / mother / feeding and being comforted, teething, sleeping	1. Trust v mistrust	Hope & drive	'cosmic order'	biological & physiological
Toddler / parents / bodily functions, toilet training, muscular control, walking	2. Autonomy v shame & doubt	Willpower & self-control	'law and order'	safety
Preschool / family / exploration and discovery, adventure and play	3. Initiative v guilt	Purpose & direction	'ideal prototypes'	belongingness & love
Schoolchild / school, teachers, friends, neighbourhood / achievement and accomplishment	4. Industry v inferiority	Competence & method	'technological elements'	esteem
Adolescent / peers, groups, influences / resolving identity and direction, becoming a grown-up	5. Identity v role confusion	Fidelity & devotion	'ideological perspectives'	esteem
Young adult / lovers, friends, work connections / intimate relationships, work and social life	6. Intimacy v isolation	Love & affiliation	'patterns of cooperation and competition'	esteem
Mid-adult / children, community / 'giving back', helping, contributing	7. Generativity v stagnation	Care & production	'currents of education and training'	self-actualisation
Late adult / society, the world, life / meaning and purpose, life achievements, acceptance	8. Integrity v despair	Wisdom & renunciation	'wisdom'	self-actualisation

We're not suggesting that there's a direct fit between Erikson's and Maslow's models, but shown together like this you can see for yourself how similar aspects could inter-relate.

You can also use Erikson's model to help explain what happens in Maslow's theory when a trauma disrupts someone's life (such as redundancy, divorce, bankruptcy or homelessness). A trauma can make an individual revisit needs and internal conflicts (crises) that were 'dealt with' years ago – but are now relevant again in the new situation. Both Erikson's and Maslow's say that anyone can find themselves revisiting and having to resolve needs, or crisis feelings or experiences from earlier years.

Erikson's model - maladaptations and malignancies (negative outcomes)

As his work progressed, Erikson refined his ideas – introducing terms like 'maladaptations' and 'malignancies' to represent the negative outcomes arising from an unhelpful experience through each of the crisis stages.

These negative outcomes are what we might call 'baggage' – the psychological outcomes of previously unhelpful experiences that people can carry with them through life. Psychoanalysis, the particular therapeutic science from which Erikson approached these issues, is a way to help people understand where the baggage came from, and help them get rid of it.

We can also have negative outcomes from repeating or revisiting a crisis – reliving the feelings we had at the time.

The chart below shows the crisis, the 'maladaptations' that can develop from tending towards the extreme of the first ('positive') disposition in each crisis, and 'malignancies' develop from tending towards the extreme of the second ('negative') disposition in each crisis.

A maladaptation could be seen as 'too much of a good thing'. A malignancy could be seen as not enough.

Erikson was careful to choose meaningful words for the maladaptations and malignancies that symbolise the emotional outcomes that are relevant to each stage.

MALADAPTATIONS AND MALIGNANCIES		
Maladaptation	Crisis	Malignancy
Sensory distortion (later sensory maladjustment)	Trust v mistrust	Withdrawal
Impulsivity (later shameless willfulness)	Autonomy v shame/doubt	Compulsion
Ruthlessness	Initiative v guilt	Inhibition
Narrow virtuosity	Industry v inferiority	Inertia
Fanaticism	Identity v role confusion	Repudiation
Promiscuity	Intimacy v isolation	Exclusivity
Overextension	Generativity v stagnation	Rejectivity
Presumption	Integrity v despair	Disdain

In each case, the maladaptation or malignancy corresponds to an extreme extension of the relevant crisis disposition (for example, 'Withdrawal' results from an extreme extension of 'Mistrust'). Thinking about this helps to understand what these outcomes entail, and interestingly helps to identify the traits in people - or oneself - when you encounter the behavioural tendency concerned.

Malignancies and maladaptations can manifest in various ways. Here are examples, using more modern and common language, to help understand and interpret the meaning and possible attitudes, tendencies, behaviours, etc., within the various malignancies and maladaptations. In each case the examples can manifest as more extreme mental difficulties, in which case the terms would be more extreme too. These examples are open to additional interpretation and are intended to be a guide, not scientific certainties. Neither do these examples suggest that anyone experiencing any of these behavioural tendencies is suffering from mental problems. Erikson never established any absolute measurement of emotional difficulty or tendency as to be defined as a malignancy or maladaptation.

MALADAPTATIONS AND MALIGNANCIES - EXAMPLES AND INTERPRETATIONS				
Examples	Maladaptation	Crisis	Malignancy	Examples
Unrealistic, spoilt, deluded	Sensory distortion	Trust v mistrust	Withdrawal	neurotic, depressive, afraid
Reckless, inconsiderate, thoughtless	Impulsivity	Autonomy v shame/doubt	Compulsion	anal, constrained, self-limiting
Exploitative, uncaring, dispassionate	Ruthlessness	initiative v guilt	Inhibition	risk-averse, unadventurous
Workaholic, obsessive specialist	Narrow virtuosity	Industry v inferiority	Inertia	lazy, apathetic, purposeless
Self-important, extremist	Fanaticism	Identity v role confusion	Repudiation	socially disconnected, cut-off
Sexually needy, vulnerable	Promiscuity	Intimacy v isolation	Exclusivity	loner, cold, self-contained
Do-gooder, busy-body, meddling	Overextension	Generativity v stagnation	Rejectivity	disinterested, cynical
Conceited, pompous, arrogant	Presumption	Integrity v despair	Disdain	miserable, unfulfilled, blaming

In truth each of us is subject to emotional feelings and extremes of various sorts, and it is always a matter of opinion as to what actually constitutes a problem. All people possess a degree of maladaptation or malignancy from each crisis experience. Not to do so would not be human, since none of us is perfect. It's always a question of degree. It's also a matter of understanding our weaknesses, maybe understanding where they come from too, and thereby better understanding how we might become stronger, more productive and happier.

Erikson's terminology

This section explains how some of the model's terminology altered as Erikson developed his theory, and is not crucial to understanding the model at a simple level.

Erikson was continually refining and re-evaluating his psychosocial theory, and he encouraged his readers and followers to do likewise. This developmental approach enabled the useful extension of the model to its current format. Some of what is summarised here did not initially appear clearly in Childhood and Society in 1950, which marked the establishment of the basic theory, not its completion. Several aspects of Erikson's theory were clarified in subsequent books decades later, including work focusing on old age by Joan Erikson, Erik's wife and collaborator, notably in the 1996 revised edition of The Life Cycle Completed: A Review.

The Eriksons' refinements also involved alterations - some would say complications - to the terminology, which (although presumably aiming for scientific precision) do not necessarily aid understanding, especially at a basic working level.

For clarity therefore this page sticks mostly with Erikson's original 1950 and other commonly used terminology. Basic Trust v Basic Mistrust (1950) is however shortened here to Trust v Mistrust, and Ego Integrity (1950) is shortened to Integrity, because these seem to be more consistent Erikson preferences. The terms used on this page are perfectly adequate, and perhaps easier too, for grasping what the theory means and making use of it.

Here are the main examples of alternative terminology that Erikson used in later works to describe the crisis stages and other aspects, which will help you recognise and understand their meaning if you see them elsewhere.

- Erikson used the terms 'syntonic' and 'dystonic' to describe the contrary dispositions and effects within each crisis stage - 'syntonic' being the 'positive' first-listed factor (e.g., Trust) and 'dystonic' being the 'negative' second-listed word (e.g., Mistrust). Again realise that a balance between syntonic and dystonic tendencies is required for healthy outcomes. Extreme tendency in either direction is not helpful. Syntonic extremes equate to maladaptations. Dystonic extremes equate to malignancies. The words syntonic and dystonic outside of Erikson's theory have quite specific scientific medical meanings which are not easy to equate to Erikson's essential ideas. Syntonic conventionally refers to a high degree of emotional response to one's environment; dystonic conventionally refers to abnormal muscular responsiveness. Neither literal definition particularly aids understanding of Erikson's theory and as such they are not very helpful in using the model.

- Erikson later used 'Adaptive Strength' as a firm description of the first disposition in each crisis, e.g., trust, autonomy, initiative. He used the description loosely early in his work but seems to have settled on it as a firm heading in later work, (notably in Vital Involvement in Old Age, 1986).

- 'Basic Virtues' Erikson also called 'Basic Strengths' (the word 'basic' generally identified the single main virtue or strength that potentially arose from each crisis, which would be accompanied by various other related strengths).

- Erikson (or maybe Joan Erikson) later used the term 'Antipathy' as an alternative for 'Malignancy' (being the negative tendency towards the second resulting from unsuccessful experience during a crisis stage).

- 'Sensory Distortion' was later referred to as 'Sensory Maladjustment', being the maladaptive tendency arising at stage one (Trust v Mistrust).

- 'Impulsivity' he later changed to 'Shameless Wilfulness', being the maladaptive tendency arising at stage two (Autonomy v Shame & Doubt)

- Erikson generally used the simpler 'Trust v Mistrust' instead of 'Basic Trust v Basic Mistrust' which first appeared in the 1950 model.

- Erikson later refined 'Industry' to 'Industriousness'.

- Erikson later referred to 'Role Confusion' as 'Identity Diffusion' and 'Identity Confusion'.

- He later referred to 'intimacy' also as 'intimacy and distantiation'. (Distantiation means the ability to bring objectivity - emotional detachment - to personal decision-making.)

- 'Ego Integrity' he also simplified at times to simply 'Integrity'.

- 'Stagnation' was later shown alternatively as 'Self-Absorption', and later still reverted to 'Stagnation'.

- At times he extended 'Despair' to 'Despair and Disgust' (Disgust here being a sort of 'sour grapes' reaction or rejective denial).

In conclusion

Erikson's psychosocial theory is very powerful for self-awareness and improvement, and for teaching and helping others.

While Erikson's model emphasises the sequential significance of the eight character-forming crisis stages, it recognises that that people continue to change and develop throughout their lives, and that personality is not exclusively formed during early childhood years. This is a helpful and optimistic idea, and many believe it is realistic too. It helps us to see the future as an opportunity for positive change and development, instead of looking back with blame and regret.

The better that people come through each crisis, the better they will tend to deal with what lies ahead. But that doesn't mean that an earlier negative experience during any of the crisis stages can't be overcome. In fact negative experiences and can be turned around if we revisit them with new insight and lessons learned.

Everyone can change and grow, no matter what has gone before. And as ever, understanding why we are like we are - gaining meaningful self-awareness - is always a useful and important step forward. Erikson's theory helps to enable this understanding and personal growth.

KANDO believes that children, parents and teachers should be taught Erikson's psychosocial theory to help all people of all ages understand the connections between life experiences and human behaviour - and particularly how grown-ups can help rather than hinder children's development into rounded emotionally mature people.

Erikson was keen to improve the way children are taught and nurtured, and KANDO thinks his ideas deserve to be more widely known and used in everyday life.

MASLOW'S HIERARCHY OF NEEDS

Maslow's Hierarchy of Needs is something you can apply in a practical way to all areas of your life. It is a simple model showing life's essentials – from concrete essentials like food and water to abstract notions like morality and creativity. All are essential for a fulfilled and happy life.

In any situation, if you or others are not satisfied and content, something must be missing. Look at the hierarchy and you will find that what was deficient in one of Maslow's core elements! You might be comfortable, well fed and have a good job but you are lonely – the missing element is family and friends. Or you might be happy and sociable bit have a yearning to do something new – your creativity is not being fulfilled. If you succeed in getting the right balance, the theory says, you will be content.

THE MOTIVATIONAL MODEL

Abraham Maslow developed his Hierarchy of Needs model in 1940 to 1950 in the US, and it remains valid today for understanding human motivation, management training, and personal development. Maslow said that the employers should provide a workplace that encourages and enables employees to fulfil their own unique potential (self-actualisation) – and idea that's as relevant as ever. Maslow's book *Motivation and Personality*, published in 1954, introduced the Hierarchy of Needs, and he extended his ideas in other work, notably his later book *Toward A Psychology Of Being*.

Abraham Maslow was born in New York in 1908 and died in 1970, although various publications appear in Maslow's name in later years. Maslow's PhD in psychology in 1934 at the University of Wisconsin formed the basis of his motivational research, initially studying rhesus monkeys.

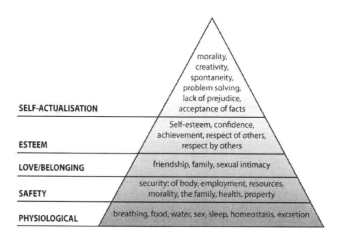

The first and simplest version of Maslow's Hierarchy of Needs five-stage model above is shown above. There were later versions with added motivational stages but they were not all clearly attributable to Maslow.

THE MODEL EXPLAINED

We are all motivated by needs. Our most basic needs are inborn, having evolved over tens of thousands of years. Abraham Maslow's Hierarchy of Needs helps to explain how these needs motivate us all.

It states that we must satisfy each need in turn, starting with the first, which deals with the most obvious needs for survival itself, such as food, water and air.

Our 'lower order' physical and emotional needs must be met first before we are concerned with the 'higher order' needs like and personal development: if someone is huddled in a refugee camp after a disaster their need for spontaneity and lack of prejudice may take a back seat!

Maslow's original Hierarchy of Needs model was first widely published in *Motivation and Personality* in 1954. This original version - which comprised five needs - remains for most people the definitive Hierarchy of Needs.

- Biological and physiological needs: air, food, drink, shelter, warmth, sex, sleep.

- Safety needs: protection from elements, security, order, law, limits, stability.

- Belongingness and love needs: work group, family, affection, relationships.

- Esteem needs: self-esteem, achievement, mastery, independence, status, dominance, prestige, managerial responsibility.

- Self-actualisation needs: realising personal potential, self-fulfilment, seeking personal growth and peak experiences.

While Maslow referred to various additional aspects of motivation, he expressed the Hierarchy of Needs in these five clear stages.

1990S ADAPTED HIERARCHY OF NEEDS INCLUDING TRANSCENDENCE NEEDS

Here's an updated version of the hierarchy:

- Biological and physiological needs - air, food, drink, shelter, warmth, sex, sleep, etc.

- Safety needs - protection from elements, security, order, law, limits, stability, etc.

- Belongingness and love needs - work group, family, affection, relationships, etc.

- Esteem needs - self-esteem, achievement, mastery, independence, status, dominance, prestige, managerial responsibility, etc.

- Cognitive needs - knowledge, meaning, etc.

- Aesthetic needs - appreciation and search for beauty, balance, form, etc.

- Self-actualisation needs - realising personal potential, self-fulfilment, seeking personal growth and peak experiences.

- Transcendence needs - helping others to achieve self-actualisation.

WHAT HIERARCHY OF NEEDS MODEL IS MOST VALID?

Abraham Maslow created the original five level Hierarchy of Needs model, and for many this remains entirely adequate for its purpose. The seven and eight level 'hierarchy of needs' models are later adaptations by others, based on Maslow's work. Arguably, the original five-level model includes the later additional sixth, seventh and eighth ('Cognitive', 'Aesthetic', and 'Transcendence') levels within the original 'Self-Actualisation' level 5, since each one of the 'new' motivators concerns an area of self-development and self-fulfilment that is rooted in self-actualisation 'growth', and is distinctly different to any of the previous 1-4 level 'deficiency' motivators. For many people, self-actualising commonly involves each and every one of the newly added drivers. As such, the original five-level Hierarchy of Needs model remains a definitive classical representation of human motivation; and the later adaptations perhaps serve best to illustrate aspects of self-actualisation.

Maslow said that needs must be satisfied in the given order. Aims and drive always shift to next higher order needs. Levels 1 to 4 are deficiency motivators; level 5, and by implication 6 to 8, are growth motivators and relatively rarely found. The thwarting of needs is usually a cause of stress, and is particularly so at level 4.

Or instance, you can't motivate someone to achieve their sales target (level 4) when they're having problems with their marriage (level 3).

MASLOW'S SELF-ACTUALISING CHARACTERISTICS

- Keen sense of reality - aware of real situations - objective judgement, rather than subjective

- See problems in terms of challenges and situations requiring solutions, rather than see problems as personal complaints or excuses

- Need for privacy and comfortable being alone

- Reliant on own experiences and judgement - independent - not reliant on culture and environment to form opinions and views

- Not susceptible to social pressures - non-conformist

- Democratic, fair and non-discriminating - embracing and enjoying all cultures, races and individual styles

- Socially compassionate - possessing humanity

- Accepting others as they are and not trying to change people

- comfortable with oneself - despite any unconventional tendencies

- A few close intimate friends rather than many surface relationships

- Sense of humour directed at oneself or the human condition, rather than at the expense of others

- Spontaneous and natural - true to oneself, rather than being how others want

- Excited and interested in everything, even ordinary things

- Creative, inventive and original

- Seek peak experiences that leave a lasting impression

See the Maslow's interviews DVDs - especially *Maslow and Self-Actualisation* to understand the subject more fully. These films were made in 1968 and are helpful on several levels, and both wonderful teaching and learning aids.

These materials also help to illustrate the far-reaching and visionary nature of Maslow's thinking, several decades ago.

The above materials are published by Maurice Bassett on behalf of the estate of Abraham Maslow. KANDO takes no commission and recommends them simply because they are wonderful materials for all students and followers of Maslow's very special work.

USING MASLOW'S HIERARCHY OF NEEDS TO UNDERSTAND BEHAVIOUR

When you first read Maslow's Hierarchy of Needs you may wonder how all of life's activities and needs can be fitted into this apparently simple model, and the truth is that to use it successfully you do need to think carefully about which behaviours relate to which sections of the model.

For example, where does 'doing things for fun' fit into the model? The answer is that it can't until you define 'doing things for fun' more accurately.

You'd need to define more precisely each given situation where a person is 'doing things for fun' in order to analyse motivation according to Maslow's Hierarchy, since the 'fun' activity motive can potentially be part any of the five original Maslow needs.

Understanding whether striving to achieve a particular need or aim is 'fun' can provide a helpful basis for identifying a Maslow driver within a given behaviour, and thereby to assess where a particular behaviour fits into the model:

- Biological - health, fitness, energising mind and body, etc.

- Safety - order and structure needs met for example by some heavily organised, structural activity

- Belongingness - team sport, club 'family' and relationships

- Esteem - competition, achievement, recognition

- Self-Actualisation drivers - challenge, new experiences, love of art, nature, etc.

However in order to relate a particular 'doing it for fun' behaviour to the Hierarchy of Needs we need to consider what makes it 'fun' (i.e., rewarding) for the person. If a behaviour is 'for fun', then consider what makes it 'fun' for the person - is the 'fun' rooted in 'belongingness', or is it from 'recognition', i.e., 'esteem'. Or is the fun at a deeper level, from the sense of self-fulfilment, i.e., 'self-actualisation'.

Apply this approach to any behaviour that doesn't immediately fit the model, and it will help you to see where it does fit.

Maslow's Hierarchy of Needs should be read and understood before you try to apply it. Although there are only five stages it's a sophisticated model and, once you get used to really examining needs and emotions, it will become easier to recognise where things 'belong' in the hierarchy.

It's generally said that – using Maslow's theory – once a need is satisfied the person moves onto the next 'layer' of needs to be fulfilled. However this can be applied too rigidly, because people and their motivations are more complex. So while it is broadly true that people move up (or down) the hierarchy, depending on what's happening to them in their lives, it is also true that at any time most people will have elements of all of the motivational drivers. For example, someone who is focused on self-actualising (level 5) will at the same time have the basic level 1 needs such as sleeping and eating. As circumstances change, so will our needs and motivations.

Maslow's theory requires some interpretation and thought. Give it time and consideration and it will help you understand and handle your emotions and behaviours and those of the people around you.

MASLOW'S HIERARCHY OF NEEDS AND HELPING OTHERS

Sometimes it's particularly hard to see how behaviour relates to Maslow's Hierarchy of Needs.

For example, normally, we would consider that selflessly helping others, as a form of personal growth motivation, would be found as part of self-actualisation, but some people seem to be far short of self-actualising, and yet are still able to help others in a meaningful and unselfish sense.

Interestingly, this concept seems to be used increasingly as an effective way to help people deal with depression, low self-esteem, poor life circumstances, etc., and it almost turns the essential Maslow model on its head: that is, by helping others, a person helps themselves to improve and develop too.

The principle has also been applied quite recently to developing disaffected school-children, who, as part of their own development, have been encouraged to 'teach' other younger children (which can arguably be interpreted as their acting at a self-actualising level - selflessly helping others). The disaffected children, theoretically striving to belong and be accepted (level 3 - belongingness) were actually remarkably good at helping other children, despite their own negative feelings and issues.

Under certain circumstances, a person striving to satisfy their needs at level 3 - belongingness, seems able to self-actualise - level 5 (and perhaps beyond, into 'transcendence') by selflessly helping others, and at the same time begins to satisfy their own needs for belongingness and self-esteem.

Such examples demonstrate the need for careful interpretation and application of the Maslow model. The Hierarchy of Needs is not a catch-all, but it does remain a wonderfully useful framework for analysing and trying to understand the subtleties - as well as the broader aspects - of human behaviour and growth.

USING PEDAGOGY

Pedagogy – leading a child to learn – is an important concept in the KANDO Emotional Intelligence programme. We've all seen how young animals learn through play and by example. A kitten pounces on its sibling's tail, practicing for the day when it will catch its prey. The mother cat shows her kittens how to hide, how to use their paws to wash behind their ears – it happens with all mammals. And it's the best way for our children to learn emotional intelligence. We need to lead and show, in a way that's fun and stimulating.

Children always ask 'why?' We need to show them why and how. We can show, through play and by example, the best way to recognise their emotions. We can teach them how to diffuse arguments, how to empathise and be good friends and how not to judge others. By doing it playfully and – vitally – by doing it with them, lessons will be learned without your child being aware of it. They'll just know that they had your full attention and that you had a good time together.

Pedagogy is a great way to teach something in an easy and fun two-way learning process.

No need to study. No need to debate. Just do and learn.

WHAT IS A PEDAGOGUE?

If you ask someone what a pedagogue is, they are likely to reply 'a teacher'. One fairly limited definition of the word pedagogue is a school teacher. Another less kind definition suggests that pedagogues are people who instruct in a dogmatic or pedantic manner. We seem to have many views on the nature of pedagogy and how it is conducted. Unfortunately, these often lead to confusion. To gain a clear understanding of pedagogy, let's look at the origin - the etymology - of the word.

The word pedagogy has its roots in ancient Greece. Rich families in ancient Greece would have many servants (often slaves), one of whom would be specifically tasked to look after the children. Often these slaves would lead or escort the children to the place of education. The Greek word for child (usually a boy) is *pais* (the stem of this is 'paid'), and leader is *agogus* - so a *paid-agogus* or pedagogue was literally a leader of children. Later, the word *pedagogue* became synonymous with the teaching of young children. Taken in this context, we would probably all agree that pedagogy is about children's education. And yet this confines us to a very limited understanding of what pedagogy is, or has the potential to become.

If we take the principle of 'leading or guiding someone to education' (derived from the Latin word *educere* –'to draw out from within), then we open up a whole new world of possibilities for learning. It's a well known aphorism: teachers teach, but educators reach – and also a principle that is at the very heart of true pedagogy. True pedagogy is far more than someone instructing. Pedagogy is leading people to a place where they can learn for themselves. It is about creating environments and situations where people can draw out from within themselves, and hone the abilities they already have, to create their own knowledge, interpret the world in their own unique ways, and ultimately realise their full potential as human beings. It's certainly not about absolutes, but is more likely to be about uncertainties. Good pedagogy is about guiding students to learning. It's about posing challenges, asking the right questions, and presenting relevant problems for learners to explore, answer and solve. True pedagogy is where educators transport their students to a place where they will be amazed by the wonders of the world they live in.

PEDAGOGY AND EDUCATION

Education is much wider than the schooling that takes place in schools or colleges.

Often – because of the way schools and colleges work – teachers have to try to cram 'schooling' into their students. The broader word 'educators' implies acting with people rather than on them.

To educate is to create and sustain informed, hopeful and respectful environments where learning can flourish. It is concerned not just with knowing about things, but also with changing ourselves and the world we live in. As such, education is a very practical activity – something that we can do for ourselves (what we could call self-education), and with others. This is a process carried out by parents and carers, friends and colleagues, and specialist educators.

PEDAGOGUES AND TEACHERS IN ANCIENT GREEK SOCIETY

Within ancient Greek society there was a strong distinction between the activities of pedagogues (paidagögus) and subject teachers (didáskalos). The first pedagogues were slaves – often foreigners and the 'spoils of war' (Young 1987). They were trusted and sometimes learned members of rich households who accompanied the sons of their 'masters' in the street, oversaw their meals, and sat beside them when being schooled. These pedagogues were generally seen as representatives of their wards' fathers and literally 'tenders' of children (pais plus agögos, a 'child-tender'). Children were often put in their charge at around seven years and remained with them until late adolescence.

THE ROLES AND RELATIONSHIPS OF PEDAGOGUES

Plato talks about pedagogues as 'men who by age and experience are qualified to serve as both leaders (hëgemonas) and custodians (paidagögous)' of children (Longenecker 1983). Their role varied but two elements were common (Smith 2006). The first was to be an accompanist or companion – carrying books and bags, and ensuring their wards were safe. The second, and more fundamental task in relation to boys, was to help them learn what it was to be men. This they did by a combination of example, conversation and disciplining. Pedagogues were moral guides who were to be obeyed (Young 1987)

The pedagogue was responsible for every aspect of the child's upbringing from correcting grammar and diction to controlling his or her sexual morals. Reciting a pedagogue's advice, Seneca said, 'Walk thus and so; eat thus and so, this is the proper conduct for a man and that for a woman; this for a married man and that for a bachelor'. (Smith 2006)

Employing a pedagogue was a custom that went far beyond Greek society. Well-to-do Romans and some Jews placed their children in the care and oversight of trusted slaves. As Young (1987) notes, it was a continuous practice from the fifth century B.C. until late into imperial times (quoted in Smith 2006). Brothers sometimes shared one pedagogue in Greek society. In contrast, in Roman society there were often several pedagogues in each family, including female overseers for girls. This tradition of accompanying and bag carrying could still be found in more recent systems of slavery such as that found in the United States.

The relation of the pedagogue to the child is a fascinating one. It brings new meaning to Friere's (1972) notion of the 'pedagogy of the oppressed' – this was the education of the privileged by the oppressed. Apparently, it was a matter that, according to Plato, did not go unnoticed by Socrates. In a conversation between Socrates and a young boy Lysis, Socrates asked, 'Someone controls you?' Lysis replied, 'Yes, he is my tutor [or pedagogue] here.' 'Is he a slave?' Socrates queried. 'Why, certainly; he belongs to us,' responded Lysis, to which Socrates mused, 'what a strange thing, I exclaimed; a free person controlled by a slave!' (Plato 1925, quoted by Smith 2006).

PEDAGOGUES AND TEACHERS

Moral supervision by the pedagogue (paidagogos) was significant in terms of status

He was more important than the schoolmaster, because the latter only taught a boy his letters, but the paidagogos taught him how to behave, a much more important matter in the eyes of his parents. He was, moreover, even if a slave, a member of the household, in touch with its ways and with the father's authority and views. The schoolmaster had no such close contact with his pupils. (Castle 1961)

However, because both pedagogues and teachers were of relatively low status they could be disrespected by the boys. There was a catch here. As the authority and position of pedagogues flowed from the head of the household, and their focus was more on life than 'letters', they had advantages over teachers (didáskalos).

The distinction between teachers and pedagogues, instruction and guidance, and education for school or life was a feature of discussions around education for many centuries. It was still around when Immanuel Kant (1724-1804) explored education. In *On Pedagogy* published in 1803, he talked as follows:

Education includes the nurture of the child and, as it grows, its culture. The latter is firstly negative, consisting of discipline; that is, merely the correcting of faults. Secondly, culture is positive, consisting of instruction and guidance (and thus forming part of education). Guidance means directing the pupil in putting into practice what he has been taught. Hence the difference between a private teacher who merely instructs, and a tutor or governor who guides and directs his pupil. The one trains for school only, the other for life. (Kant 1900)

So how did 'pedagogy' become focused on teaching?

THE GROWING FOCUS ON TEACHING

In Europe concern with the process and content of teaching and instruction developed significantly in the sixteenth and seventeenth centuries. It was, however, part of a movement that dated from 300-400 years earlier. In the sixteenth and seventeenth centuries we see, for example:

- A growing literature about instruction and method aimed at schoolteachers.

- The grouping together of different areas of knowledge in syllabi which set out what was to be instructed.

- A focus on the organisation and development of schools (Hamilton 1999).

There was a 'the separation of the activity of 'teaching' from the activity of defining 'that which is taught'. This led in much of continental Europe to a growing interest in the process of teaching and the gathering together of examples, guidance and knowledge in the form of what became known as didactics.

DIDACTICS

Didactics helps open people's minds to new ideas. It's a way of teaching fully and comprehensively in the best possible way.

John Amos Comenius's published his great work on didactics, *The Great Didactic [Didactica Magna]* in 1648. In it he defined the principle of Didactica Magna, *omnis, omnia, omnino* – to teach everything to everybody thoroughly, in the best possible way. Comenius believed that everyone should strive for perfection in all of life's essentials and do this as thoroughly as possible. Every person must strive to become a rational being, a person who can rule nature and him or herself, and a being mirroring the creator. (Gundem 1992).

He developed sets of rules for teaching and set out basic principles. His fundamental conclusions, according to Gundem 1992) remain valid:

- Teaching must be in accordance with the student's stage of development.

- All learning happens through the senses.

- One should proceed from the specific to the general, from what is easy to the more difficult, from what is known to the unknown.

- Teaching should not cover too many subjects or themes at the same time.

- Teaching should proceed slowly and systematically. Nature makes no jumps.

Following Kant and Comenius, another significant turning point in thinking about teaching came through the growing influence of one of Kant' successors in the Chair of Philosophy at Königsberg University: Johann Friedrich Herbart (1776-1841).

THEORIES OF TEACHING

As Hamilton (1999) has put it, Herbart sought to devise, from first principles, an educational system and thus worked towards a general theory of pedagogics.

At the centre of his theory of education and of schooling is the idea of 'educational teaching' or 'educating instruction'.

Like practical and theoretical educationalists before him, Herbart also makes a distinction between education and teaching. 'Education' means shaping the development of character with a view to the improvement of man. 'Teaching' represents the world, conveys fresh knowledge, develops existing aptitudes and imparts useful skills....

Before Herbart, it was unusual to combine the concepts of 'education' and 'teaching'. Consequently, questions pertaining to education and teaching were initially pursued independently... Herbart... took the bold step of 'subordinating' the concept of 'teaching' to that of 'education' in his educational theory. As he saw it, external influences, such as the punishment or shaming of pupils, were not the most important instruments of education. On the contrary, appropriate teaching was the only sure means of promoting education that was bound to prove successful.

In Herbart's own words, teaching is the 'central activity of education'.

What Herbart and his followers achieved with this was to focus consideration of instruction and teaching (didactics) around schooling rather than other educational settings (Gundem 2000). Herbart also turned didactics 'into a discipline of its own' – extracting it from general educational theory. Simplified and rather rigid versions of his approach grew in influence with the development of mass schooling and state-defined curricula.

This approach did not go unchallenged at the time. There were those who argued that teaching should become part of the human rather than 'exact' sciences (see Hamilton 1999: 145-6). Rather than seeking to construct detailed systems of instruction, the need was to explore the human experience of teaching, learning and schooling. It was through educational practice and reflection upon it ('learning by doing') and exploring the settings in which it happens that greater understanding would develop. In Germany some of those arguing against an over-focus on method and state control of curricula looked to social pedagogy with its focus on community and democracy.

EDUCATION AS A SCIENCE

These ideas found their way across the channel and into English-language books and manuals about teaching – especially those linked to Herbart, but its influence was not wide. In 1981 Brian Simon wrote 'Why no pedagogy in England?', arguing that with changes in schooling in the latter years of the nineteenth century and growing government intervention there was much less emphasis upon on intellectual growth and much more on containment. In addition the psychology upon which it was based was increasingly called into question.

He said the most striking aspect of current thinking and discussion about education is its eclectic character, reflecting deep confusion of thought, and of aims and purposes, relating to learning and teaching – to pedagogy.

As a result, education as a science – and its study – is 'still less a 'science' and has little prestige. He continued: 'The dominant educational institutions of this country have had no concern with theory, its relation to practice, with pedagogy' (he defined pedagogy as the science of teaching). More recently, educationalists like Robin Alexander have argued that it is the prominence of curriculum in English schooling led to pedagogy (as the process of teaching) remaining in a subsidiary position

THE RE-EMERGENCE OF PEDAGOGY

In continental Europe interest in didactics and pedagogy remained relatively strong and there were significant debates and developments in thinking. But relatively little attention was paid to pedagogy in Britain and north America until the 1970s and early 1980s.

WRITING ABOUT PEDAGOGY

Initially, interest in pedagogy was reawakened by the decision of Paulo Freire to name his influential book *Pedagogy of the Oppressed* (first published in English in 1970). The book became a key reference point on many education programmes in higher education and central to the establishment of explorations around critical pedagogy. It was followed another pivotal text – Basil Bernstein's (1971) 'On the classification and framing of educational knowledge'. He drew upon developments in continental debates. He then placed them in relation to the different degrees of control people had over their lives and educational experience according to their class position and cultures. Later he was to look at messages carried by different pedagogies (Bernstein 1990). Last, we should not forget the influence of Jerome Bruner's discussion of the culture of education (1996). He argued that teachers need to pay particular attention to the cultural contexts in which they are working and of the need to look to 'folk theories' and 'folk pedagogies' (Bruner 1996). 'Pedagogy is never innocent', he wrote, 'It is a medium that carries its own message'.

PEDAGOGY AS A MEANS OF CONTROL

A fundamental element in the growing interest in pedagogy was a shift in government focus in education in England. As well as seeking to control classroom activity via the curriculum there was a movement to increase the monitoring of classroom activity via regular scrutiny by senior leadership teams and a much enhanced Ofsted evaluation schedule for lesson observation (Ofsted 2011; 2012). Key indicators for classroom observation included a variety of learning styles addressed, pace, dialogue, the encouragement of independent learning and so on (Ofsted 2011). A number of popular guides appeared to help teachers on their way – perhaps the best received of which was *The Perfect Ofsted Lesson* (Beere 2010). While the language sounded progressive, and the practices promoted had merit, the problem was the framework in which it was placed. It was, to use Alexander's words, 'pedagogy of compliance'. 'You may be steeped in educational research and/or the accumulated wisdom of 40 years in the classroom, but unless you defer to all this official material your professional judgements will be 'uninformed" (Alexander 2004)

PEDAGOGY OR DIDACTICS

Unfortunately, the way pedagogy was being defined still looked back to the focus on teaching that Herbart argued for nearly 200 years ago. For example, the now defunct General Teaching Council for England, described it as:

Pedagogy is the stuff of teachers' daily lives. Put simply it's about teaching. But we take a broad view of teaching as a complex activity, which encompasses more than just 'delivering' education. Another way to explain it is by referring to:

- The art of teaching – the responsive, creative, intuitive part

- The craft of teaching – skills and practice

- The science of teaching – research-informed decision making and the theoretical underpinning.

It is also important to remember that all these are grounded in ethical principles and moral commitment – teaching is never simply an instrumental activity, a question just of technique.

While we can welcome the warnings against viewing teaching as an instrumental activity – whether it is satisfactory to describe it as pedagogy is a matter for some debate. Indeed Hamilton (1999) has argued that much of what passes for pedagogy in UK education debates is better understood as didactics. We can see this when looking at the following description of didactics from Künzli (1994 quoted in Gundem 2000).

Simplified we may say that the concerns of didactics are: what should be taught and learned (the content aspect); how to teach and learn (the aspects of transmitting and learning): to what purpose or intention something should he taught and learnt (the goal/aims aspect

Perhaps because the word 'didactic' in the English language is associated with dull 'fill the pupils with information' forms of teaching, those wanting to develop schooling tended to avoid using it. Yet, in many respects, key aspects of what is talked about today as pedagogy in the UK and north America are better approached via this continental tradition of didactics.

PEDAGOGY AS ACCOMPANYING, CARING FOR (AND ABOUT) AND BRINGING LEARNING TO LIFE

A third element in the turn to pedagogy came from concerns in social work and youth work in the UK that the needs of many children were not being met by existing forms of practice and provision. Significantly, a number of practitioners and academics looked to models of practice found in continental Europe and Scandinavia and focused, in particular, on the traditions of social pedagogy (see Lorenz 1994; Smith 1999; Cameron 2004 and Cameron and Moss 2011). In Scotland, for example, there was discussion of the 'Scottish pedagogue' (after the use of the term 'Danish pedagogue) (Cohen 2008).

In England various initiatives and discussions emerged around reconceptualising working with children in care as social pedagogy and similarly the activities of youth workers, teachers, mentors and inclusion workers within schools (see, for example, Kyriacou's work 2010).

Significantly, much of this work bypassed the English language discussion of pedagogy – which was probably an advantage in some ways. However, it also missed just how much work in the UK was undertaken by specialist pedagogues drawing upon thinking and practice well-known to social pedagogues but whose identity has been formed around youth work, informal and social education and community learning and development (Smith 1999, 2009).

If we look to these traditions we are likely to re-appreciate pedagogy. It can be seen as what we need to know, the skills we need to command, and the commitments we need to live in order to make and justify the many different kinds of decisions needed to be made.

A FOCUS ON FLOURISHING

Pedagogues have a fundamentally different focus to subject teachers. Their central concern is with the well-being of those they are among and with. In many respects, as Kerry Young (1999) has argued with regard to youth work, pedagogues are involved for much of the time in an exercise in moral philosophy. Those they are working with are frequently seeking to answer in some way profound questions about themselves and the situations they face. At root these look to how people should live their lives: 'what is the right way to act in this situation or that; what makes me and others; how should I to relate to people; what sort of society should I be working for?' (Smith and Smith 2008). At the same time, pedagogues need to look inwards and reflect on what might make for flourishing and happiness (in Aristotle's terms *eudaimonia*).

In looking to continental concerns and debates around pedagogy, a number of specialist pedagogues have turned to the work of Pestalozzi and to those concerned with more holistic forms of practice (see, for example, Cameron and Ross 2011). As Brühlmeier (2010: 5) has commented, 'Pestalozzi has shown that there is more to [education] than attaining prescribed learning outcomes; it is concerned with the whole person, with their physical, mental and psychological development'. Learning is a matter of head, hand and heart. Heart here is a matter of 'spirit – the passions that animate or move us; moral sense or conscience – the values, ideals and attitudes that guide us; and being – the kind of person we are, or wish to be, in the world (Doyle and Smith 1999).

THE PERSON OF THE PEDAGOGUE

This is a way of working that is deeply wrapped up with the person of the pedagogue and their ability to reflect, make judgements and respond (Smith and Smith 2008). They need to be experienced as people who can be trusted, respected and turned to.

We are called upon to be wise. We are expected to hold truth dearly, to be sincere and accurate. There is also, usually, an expectation that we have a good understanding of the subjects upon which we are consulted, and that we know something about the way of the world. We are also likely to be approached for learning and counsel if we are seen as people who have the ability to come to sound judgements, and to help others to see how they may act for the best in different situations, and how they should live their lives. (Smith and Smith 2008).

At one level, the same could be said of a 'good' subject teacher in a school. As Palmer (1998) has argued, 'good teaching cannot be reduced to technique; good teaching comes from the identity and integrity of the teacher'. However, the focus of pedagogues frequently takes them directly into questions around identity and integrity. This then means that their authenticity and the extent to which they are experienced as wise are vital considerations.

THE IMPORTANCE OF 'BEING THERE'

The image of Greek pedagogues walking alongside their charges, or sitting with them in classrooms is a powerful one. It connects directly with the experiences of many care workers, youth workers, support workers and informal educators. They spend a lot of time being part of other people's lives – sometimes literally walking with them to some appointment or event, or sitting with them in meetings and sessions. They also can be a significant person for someone over a long period of time – going through difficulties and achievements with them. Green and Christian (1998) have descried this as 'accompanying'.

The greatest gift that we can give is to 'be alongside' another person. It is in times of crisis or achievement or when we have to manage long-term difficulties that we appreciate the depth and quality of having another person to accompany us. In Western society at the end of the twentieth century this gift has a fairly low profile. Although it is pivotal in establishing good communities its development is often left to chance and given a minor status compared with such things as management structure and formal procedures. But this sort of quality companionship and support is vital for people to establish and maintain their physical, mental and spiritual health and creativity.

It is easy to overlook the sophistication of this relationship and the capacities needed to be 'alongside another'. It entails 'being with' – and this involves attending to the other.

Teaching and guiding young people is based on good relationships, and these relationships can 'develop only when the persons involved pay attention to one another' (Barry and Connolly 1986). Working with individual young people is highly skilled work, drawing on, through different stages in the process, a range of diverse roles and capacities. Done well the teacher or pedagogue moves seamlessly through the stages, but the unifying core is the relationship between young person and the worker. (Collander-Brown 2005).

As a pedagogue, you must be available and prepared to respond to the emergencies of life – little and large (Smith and Smith 2008).

CARING FOR AND CARING ABOUT

Our understanding of what is involved in 'caring' has been greatly enhanced by the work of Nel Noddings. She distinguishes between 'caring for' and' caring about'. Caring for involves face-to-face encounters in which one person attends directly to the needs of another. As children, we learn first what it means to be cared-for. 'Then, gradually, we learn both to care for and, by extension, to care about, others' (Noddings 2002). Such caring about, Noddings suggests, can be seen as providing the foundation for our sense of justice.

Noddings then argues that caring relations are a foundation for pedagogical activity (by which she means teaching activity).

First, as we listen to our students, we gain their trust. Then, in an on-going relationship of care and trust, it is more likely that our students will accept what we try to teach. They will not see our efforts as 'interference' but, rather, as co-operative work proceeding from the integrity of the relation. Second, as we engage our students in dialogue, we learn about their needs, working habits, interests, and talents. We gain important ideas from them about how to build our lessons and plan for their individual progress. Finally, as we acquire knowledge about our students' needs and realise how much more than the standard curriculum is needed, we are inspired to increase our own competence (Noddings 2005).

For many of those concerned with social pedagogy it is a place where care and education meet – one is not somehow less than the other (Cameron and Moss 2011). For example, in Denmark 'care' can be seen as one of the four central areas that describe the pedagogical tasks:

Care (take care of), socialisation (to and in communities), formation (for citizenship and democracy) and learning (development of individual skills). The 'pedagogical' task is not simply about development, but also about looking after. Pedagogues not only put the individual child in the centre, but also take care of the interests of the community. (BUPL undated).

This helping relationship 'involves listening and exploring issues and problems with people; and teaching and giving advice; and providing direct assistance; and being seen as people of integrity'. (Smith and Smith 2008).

BRINGING LEARNING TO LIFE

In talking about pedagogy as a process of bringing learning to life we focus on three aspects. Pedagogy as:

- Animation: bringing 'life' into situations. This is often achieved through offering new experiences.

- Reflection: creating moments and spaces to explore lived experience.

- Action: working with people so that they are able to make changes in their lives.

Animation

In their 1997 book *Working with experience: Animating learning* David Boud and Nod Miller link 'animating' to 'learning' because of the word's connotations: to give life to, to quicken, to vivify, to inspire. They see the job of animators (animateurs) to be that of 'acting with learners, or with others, in situations where learning is an aspect of what is occurring, to assist them to work with their experience' (1997). It is a pretty good description of what many social pedagogues, youth workers and informal educators do for much of the time. They work with people on situations and relationships so that they are more stimulating and satisfying. However, they also look to what Dewey (1916) described as enlarging experience and to making it more vivid and inspiring (to use Boud and Miller's words). They encourage people to try new things and provide opportunities that open up fresh experiences.

Reflection

Within these fields of practice there has been a long-standing tradition of looking to learning from experience and, thus, to encouraging reflection (see, for example, Smith 1994). Conversation is central to the practice of informal educators and animators of community learning and development. With this has come a long tradition of starting and staying with the concerns and interests of those they are working with, while at the same time creating moments and spaces where people can come to know themselves, their situations and what is possible in their lives and communities.

Action

This isn't learning that stops at the classroom door, but is focused around working with people so that they can make changes in their lives – and in communities. As Lindeman put it many years ago, this is education as life. Based in responding to 'situations, not subjects' (1926), it involves a committed and action-oriented form of education. This:

... is not formal, not conventional, not designed merely for the purpose of cultivating skills, but... something which relates [people] definitely to their community... It has for one of its purposes the improvement of methods of social action... We are people who want change but we want it to be rational, understood. (Lindeman 1951)

In short, this is a process of joining in with people's lives and working with them to make informed and committed change.

CONCLUSION

The growing interest in social pedagogy and specialist pedagogues in some countries, when put alongside developments in thinking about the nature of learning, means that we are at one of those moments where there might be movement around how the term is used in English-language contexts. We can ask:

- Is pedagogy tied to age?

- Can the notion of pedagogy be unhooked from the discourse of schooling and returned to something more like its Greek origins?

- Where are we to stand in the debate around whether it is an art, science or craft?

JUST FOR CHILDREN?

As we have seen, the word pedagogy' is derived from the Greek and translates as 'to lead the child' or 'tend the child'. In common usage it is often used to describe practice with children. Indeed, much of the work that 'social pedagogy' has been used to describe has been with children and young people. While Paulo Freire (1972) and others talked about pedagogy in relation to working with adults, there are plenty who argue that it cannot escape its roots is bound up with practice with children. For example, Malcolm Knowles (1970) was convinced that adults learned differently to children – and that this provided the basis for a distinctive field of enquiry. He, thus, set andragogy – the art and science' of helping adults learn – against pedagogy.

While we might question whether children's processes of learning differ significantly from adults, it is the case that educators tend to approach them differently and employ contrasting strategies. The question we are left with is whether it is more helpful to restrict usage of the term 'pedagogy' to practice with children or whether it can be applied across the age range? There is a fairly strong set of arguments for the former position – the word's origin; organisational and policy concerns that tend separate children (up to 18 years old) from adults; and current usage of the term. Against restricting it to children are that learning isn't easily divided along child/adult lines; and via writers like Freire it is possible to draw on traditions of thinking and practice regarding pedagogy that apply to both adults and children. While recognizing the strength of the arguments for using 'pedagogy to describe practice across the lifespan, there may be pragmatic reasons for retaining a focus on children and young people. In part this flows from the organisational context of schooling, welfare and education service; in part from etymology.

PEDAGOGY AND SCHOOLING

There are also questions around the extent to which, in the English language at least, the notion of pedagogy has been tainted by its association with schooling. When we use the term to what extent are we importing assumptions and practices that we may not intend? 'At the heart of this language', wrote as Street and Street (1991), 'in contemporary society, there is a relentless commitment to instruction'. While didactics may be the most appropriate or logical way of thinking about the processes, ideas and commitments involved in teaching, there is some doubt that the term 'pedagogy' can take root in any sensible way in debates where English is the dominant language.

In Britain and Ireland there is some hope that pedagogy can be rescued. That possibility rests largely on the extent to which social pedagogy and its associated forms become established – especially in social work and community learning and development. If this professional identity takes root, and academic training programmes follow, then there is a chance that a counter-culture will grow and offer a contrasting set of debates. There is some evidence that this is beginning to happen with jobs with the social pedagogue title appearing in both care settings and schools, and new degree programmes being established in the UK.

ART, SCIENCE OR CRAFT?

Some say that pedagogy can be approached as a science (see, for example, the discussions in Kornbeck and Jensen 2009), while others look to it more as an art or craft. Donald Schön's (1983) work on reflective practice and his critique of the sort of 'technical rationality' that has been crudely employed within more 'scientific' approaches to practice has been influential. Elliot Eisner's (1979) view of education and teaching as improvisatory and having a significant base in process has also been looked to. He argued that the ability to reflect, imagine and respond involves developing 'the ideas, the sensibilities, the skills, and the imagination to create work that is well proportioned, skilfully executed, and imaginative, regardless of the domain in which an individual works'. 'The highest accolade we can confer upon someone', he continued, 'is to say that he or she is an artist whether as a carpenter or a surgeon, a cook or an engineer, a physicist or a teacher'

The idea of pedagogy and teaching as a craft got a significant boost in the 1990s through the work of Brown and McIntyre (1993). Their research showed, that day-to-day, the work of experienced teachers had a strong base in what is best described as a 'craft knowledge' of ideas, routines and situations. In much the same way that C Wright Mills talked of 'intellectual craftsmanship', so we can think of pedagogy as involving certain commitments and processes.

Scholarship is a choice of how to live as well as a choice of career; whether he knows it or not, the intellectual workman forms his own self as he works toward the perfection of his craft; to realize his own potentialities, and any opportunities that come his way, he constructs a character which has as its core the qualities of a good workman.

What this means is that you must learn to use your life experience in your intellectual work: continually to examine and interpret it. In this sense craftsmanship is the centre of yourself and you are personally involved in every intellectual product upon which you work. (Mills 1959)

There is a significant overlap between what Schön talks about as artistry and Mills as craftsmanship – and many specialist pedagogues within the UK would be much more at home with these ways of describing their activities, than as a science. Certainly, it is difficult to see how the environments or conditions in which pedagogues work can be measured and controlled in the same way that would be normal in what we might call 'science'. It is also next to impossible on a day-to-day basis to assess in a scientific way the different influences on an individual and group, and the extent to which the work of the pedagogue made a difference.

We need to move discussions of pedagogy beyond seeing it as primarily being about teaching – and look at those traditions of practice that flow from the original pedagogues in ancient Greece. We have much to learn through exploring through the thinking and practice of specialist pedagogues who look to accompany learners; care for and about them; and bring learning into life. Teaching is just one aspect of their practice.

LEV SEMYONOVICH VYGOTSKY

Lev Semyonovich Vygotsky was the world's expert on Language Scaffolding, which studies the importance of the words we use to describe things we want others to understand.

Vygotsky's main work was in developmental psychology. His theory of the development of higher cognitive functions in children said that reasoning emerges through practical activity in a social environment. He argued that the development of reasoning was mediated by signs and symbols, and so depended on the culture and language surrounding child as well as on universal cognitive processes.

He discussed the Zone of Proximal Development, often understood to refer to the way in which the acquisition of new knowledge is dependent on previous learning, as well as the availability of instruction.

Vygotsky's theories were controversial within the Soviet Union and after his ideas were introduced in the west in the 1930 they remained virtually unknown until the 1970s when they became a central component of the development of new paradigms in developmental and educational psychology. His theories are widely known today, although scholars do not always agree with them, or agree about what he meant. More recently, understandings of many of Vygotsky's central concepts and theories has been re-evaluated.

SCIENTIFIC LEGACY

Vygotsky was a pioneering psychologist and his major works span six separate volumes, written over roughly 10 years, from *Psychology of Art* (1925) to *Thought and Language* [or *Thinking and Speech*] (1934). Vygotsky's interests in the fields of developmental psychology, child development, and education were extremely diverse. His philosophical framework includes insightful interpretations of the cognitive role of mediation tools, as well as the re-interpretation of well-known concepts in psychology such as internalisation of knowledge. Vygotsky introduced the notion of zone of proximal development, an innovative metaphor capable of describing the potential of human cognitive development.

His work covered such diverse topics as the origin and the psychology of art, development of higher mental functions, philosophy of science and methodology of psychological research, the relation between learning and human development, concept formation, interrelation between language and thought development, play as a psychological phenomenon, learning disabilities, and abnormal human development (aka defectology). His scientific thinking underwent several major transformations throughout his career, but generally Vygotsky's legacy can be divided into two fairly distinct periods and the transitional phase between the two during which Vygotsky experienced the crisis in his theory and personal life. These are the mechanistic 'instrumental' period of the 1920s, integrative 'holistic' period of 1930s, and the transitional years of, roughly, 1929-1931. Each of these periods is characterised by its distinct themes and theoretical innovations.

THOUGHT AND LANGUAGE

Perhaps Vygotsky's most important contribution concerns the inter-relationship of language development and thought. This concept, explored in Vygotsky's book *Thought and Language*, (Russian: *Myshlenie i rech*, alternative translation: *Thinking and Speaking*) establishes the explicit and profound connection between speech (both silent inner speech and oral language), and the development of mental concepts and cognitive awareness. Vygotsky described inner speech as being qualitatively different from normal (external) speech. Although Vygotsky believed inner speech developed from external speech via a gradual process of internalisation, with younger children only really able to 'think out loud,' he claimed that, in its mature form, inner speech would be unintelligible to anyone except the thinker, and would not resemble spoken language as we know it (in particular, being greatly compressed). Hence, thought itself develops socially.

Language starts as a tool external to the child used for social interaction. The child guides personal behavior by using this tool in a kind of self-talk or 'thinking out loud.' Initially, self-talk is very much a tool of social interaction and this tapers to negligible levels when the child is alone or with deaf children. Gradually, self-talk is used more as a tool for self-directed and self-regulating behaviour. Because speaking has been appropriated and internalised, self-talk is no longer present around the time the child starts school. Self-talk 'develops along a rising not a declining, curve; it goes through an evolution, not an involution. In the end, it becomes inner speech' (Vygotsky, 1987).

Speaking has thus developed along two lines: the line of social communication and the line of inner speech, by which the child mediates and regulates his or her activity through their thoughts. The thoughts, in turn, are mediated by the semiotics (the meaningful signs) of inner speech. This is not to say that thinking cannot take place without language, but rather that it is mediated by it and thus develops to a much higher level of sophistication.

ZONE OF PROXIMAL DEVELOPMENT

'Zone of proximal development' (ZPD) is Vygotsky's term for the range of tasks that a child is in the process of learning to complete. The lower limit of ZPD is the level of skill reached by the child working independently (also referred to as the child's actual developmental level). The upper limit is the level of potential skill that the child is able to reach with the assistance of a more capable instructor.

Vygotsky viewed the ZPD as a way to better explain the relation between children's learning and cognitive development. Before the ZPD, there were three main theories about the relation between learning and development: 1) Development always precedes learning (e.g., constructivism): children first need to meet a particular maturation level before learning can occur; 2) Learning and development cannot be separated but instead occur simultaneously (e.g., behaviourism): essentially, learning is development; and 3) learning and development are separate but interactive processes (e.g., gestaltism): one process always prepares the other process, and vice versa. Vygotsky rejected these three major theories because he believed that learning always precedes development in the ZPD. In other words, through the assistance of a more capable person, a child is able to learn skills or aspects of a skill that go beyond the child's actual developmental or maturational level. Therefore, development always follows the child's potential to learn. In this sense, the ZPD provides a prospective view of cognitive development, as opposed to a retrospective view that characterises development in terms of a child's independent capabilities.

'Scaffolding' is a concept closely related to the idea of ZPD, although Vygotsky never actually used the term. Scaffolding is changing the level of support to suit the cognitive potential of the child so the appropriate level of guidance is always applied. Over the course of a teaching session, a more skilled person adjusts the amount of guidance to fit the child's potential level of performance. More support is offered when a child is having difficulty with a particular task and, over time, less support is provided as the child makes gains on the task. Ideally, scaffolding works to maintain the child's potential level of development in the ZPD. An essential element to the ZPD and scaffolding is the acquisition of language. According to Vygotsky, language (and in particular, speech) is fundamental to children's cognitive growth because language provides purpose and intention so that behaviours can be better understood. Through the use of speech, children are able to communicate to and learn from others through dialogue, which is an important tool in the ZPD. In a dialogue, a child's unsystematic, disorganised, and spontaneous concepts are met with the more systematic, logical and rational concepts of the skilled helper. Empirical research suggests that the benefits of scaffolding are not only useful during a task, but can extend beyond the immediate situation in order to influence future cognitive development. For instance, a recent study recorded 'verbal scaffolding' between mothers and their three- and four-year-old children as they played together. Then, when the children were six years old, they underwent several measures of executive function, such as working memory and goal-directed play. The study found that the children's working memory and language skills at six years of age were related to the amount of verbal scaffolding provided by mothers at age three. In particular, scaffolding was most effective when mothers provided explicit conceptual links during play. The results of this study not only suggest that verbal scaffolding aids children's cognitive development, but that the quality of the scaffolding is also important for learning and development.

PSYCHOLOGY OF PLAY

Vygotsky realised the importance of play and children's games, as a psychological phenomenon and its role in the child's development. Through play the child develops abstract meaning separate from the objects in the world, which is a critical feature in the development of higher mental functions. Vygotsky gives the famous example of a child who wants to ride a horse but cannot. If the child were under three, he would perhaps cry and be angry, but around the age of three the child's relationship with the world changes:

After this age, Vygotsky said, play is the imaginary, illusory realisation of unrealisable desires. Imagination is a new formation that is not present in the consciousness of the very raw young child, is totally absent in animals, and represents a specifically human form of conscious activity. Like all functions of consciousness, it originally arises from action.

The child wishes to ride a horse but cannot, said Vygotsky, so he picks up a stick and stands astride it, pretending he is riding a horse. The stick is a pivot. 'Action according to rules begins to be determined by ideas, not by objects... It is terribly difficult for a child to sever thought (the meaning of a word) from object. Play is a transitional stage in this direction. At that critical moment when a stick – i.e., an object – becomes a pivot for severing the meaning of horse from a real horse, one of the basic psychological structures determining the child's relationship to reality is radically altered'.

As children get older, their reliance on pivots such as sticks, dolls and other toys diminishes. They have internalised these pivots as imagination and abstract concepts through which they can understand the world. 'The old adage that 'children's play is imagination in action' can be reversed: we can say that imagination in adolescents and schoolchildren is play without action'.

Vygotsky also referred to the development of social rules that form, for example, when children play house and adopt the roles of different family members. Vygotsky cites an example of two sisters playing being sisters. The rules of behaviour between them that go unnoticed in daily life are consciously acquired through play. As well as social rules, the child acquires what we now refer to as self-regulation. For example, when a child stands at the starting line of a running race, she may well desire to run immediately so as to reach the finish line first, but her knowledge of the social rules surrounding the game and her desire to enjoy the game enable her to regulate her initial impulse and wait for the start signal.

WHERE DO WE START WITH EI?

Now we have the frameworks to use and relate to, where do we start? The best place to begin is by taking the expert knowledge of Erikson, Maslow, Vygotsky and others and applying it to your particular situation. In helping your child to learn how to recognise and use their EI, you can choose the elements of the framework that are most relevant to you and your teaching style.

SELF-TEACHING EI

All information to our brain comes through our senses. When this information is overwhelmingly emotional or stressful our instinct will take over. As a result our ability to act will be limited to the flight, fight or freeze response. We need to be able to bring our emotions into balance at will so that we have access to a wide range of choices and the ability to make good decisions.

Also strongly linked to emotion is memory. If we can learn to stay connected to the emotional part of our brain as well as the rational we will expand our range of choices when it comes to responding to a new event. It will also help us factor in emotional memory into the decision-making process. This will help prevent continually repeating earlier mistakes.

To improve both emotional intelligence and decision making abilities we need to understand and manage our emotions. This can be achieved by developing key skills for controlling and managing stress and becoming an effective communicator.

By reducing stress, remaining focused and staying connected to oneself and others Emotional Intelligence can be built. This can be done by learning key skills.

The first two skills are essential for controlling and managing stress and the last three improve communication. Each skill builds on the lessons learned in practicing the earlier skills and include:

- The ability to quickly reduce stress in the moment in a variety of settings

- The ability to recognise your emotions and keep them from overwhelming you

- The ability to connect emotionally with others by using non-verbal communication

- The ability to use humour and play to stay connected in challenging situations

- The ability to resolve conflicts positively and with confidence.

The key skills of Emotional Intelligence can be learned by anyone at any time. There is, however, a large difference between learning about EI and applying that knowledge in your life. Simply knowing you should do something does not mean you will, especially when overwhelmed by stress which can hijack the best of intentions.

To change behaviour in ways that can stand up to pressure it is necessary to learn how to overcome stress in the moment and stress in relationships by remaining emotionally aware. But just reading about EI isn't enough – you also have to experience and practice the skills in everyday life.

SKILL 1: REDUCE STRESS IN THE MOMENT

Being able to quickly calm yourself down and relieve stress helps you stay balanced, focused and in control, no matter what challenges you face or how stressful a situation becomes.

Develop stress-busting skills by working through the following steps:

- Realise when you are stressed. The first step in reducing stress is to recognise what stress feels like. How does your body feel? Are your muscles or stomach tight? Are your hands clenched? Is your breath shallow? Being aware of your own individual physical response to stress will help regulate tension when it occurs.

- Identify your stress response. Everyone reacts differently to stress. If you become agitated or angry under stress the most successful stress-relieving activities will be those that calm you down. But if you tend to become depressed or withdrawn you will respond best to stress-relieving activities that are stimulating. If you tend to freeze – speeding up in some ways while slowing down in others - you need stress-relieving activities that provide both comfort and stimulation.

- Discover the stress-busting activities that work for you. The most effective way to reduce stress quickly is by engaging one or more of your senses – sight, sound, smell, taste and touch. As each person responds differently to sensory input you need to find things that are soothing and/or energising to you.

SKILL 2: BEAT RELATIONSHIP STRESS WITH EMOTIONAL AWARENESS

The key to understanding yourself and remaining calm and focused in tense situations with others is being able to connect to your emotions. That means having a moment-to-moment awareness of your emotions and how they influence your thoughts and actions.

Many people are disconnected from their emotions, particularly the strong core emotions such as anger, sadness, fear and joy. We may be able to distort, deny or numb our feelings but we cannot eliminate them. They are still there, although whether we are aware of them or not. Without emotional intelligence we are unable to fully understand our own motivations and needs or to communicate effectively with others. Also we are at a much greater risk of becoming overwhelmed in situations that appear threatening.

What kind of relationship do you have with your emotions?

- Do you experience feelings that flow, encountering one emotion after another as your experiences change from one moment to another?

- Are your emotions accompanied by physical sensations that you experience in places like your stomach or your chest?

- Do you experience discreet identifiable feelings and emotions, such as anger, sadness, fear, joy, each of which is evident in subtle facial expressions?

- Can you experience intense feeling that are strong enough to capture both your attention and that of others?

- Do you pay attention to your emotions? Do they factor into your decision making?

If any of the above experiences are unfamiliar, your emotions may be turned down or turned off. To be emotionally healthy and emotionally intelligent you must reconnect to your core emotions, accept them and become comfortable with them.

SKILL 3: NON-VERBAL COMMUNICATION

Being an effective communicator is more than just verbal skills and the ability to manage stress. What you say can be less important than how you say it. These are the non-verbal signals you send out – the gestures you make, the way you sit, how fast or loud you talk, how close you stand to others or how much eye contact you make. To hold the attention of others and build connections and trust you need to be aware of, and in control of, your body language. Also you need to be able to accurately read and respond to the non-verbal cues that people send you.

Non-verbal messages do not stop when you stop talking; when you are silent you are still communicating non-verbally. Non-verbal messages can produce a sense of interest, trust, excitement and desire for connection. Or they can generate fear, confusion, distrust and disinterest.

Tips for improving non-verbal communication

Successful and appropriate non-verbal communication depends on your ability to manage stress, recognise your own emotions and understand the signals you are both sending and receiving.

When communicating:

- Focus on the other person. Be attentive – if you are planning what you are going to say next, daydreaming or thinking about something else you are almost certain to miss non-verbal cues and other subtleties in the conversation.

- Make eye contact. Eye contact can communicate interest, maintain the flow of a conversation, and help gauge the other person's response.

- Pay attention to non-verbal cues you are both sending and receiving, such as facial expression, tone of voice, posture and gestures, touch and the timing and pace of your conversation.

SKILL 4: USE HUMOUR AND PLAY TO DEAL WITH CHALLENGES

Humour, laughter and play are natural antidotes to life's difficulties. They can lighten burdens and help you keep things in perspective.

Laughter can reduce stress, elevate mood and bring the nervous system back into balance.

Playful communication broadens emotional intelligence and helps you:

- Take hardships in your stride. By allowing you to view your frustrations and disappointments from new perspectives, laughter and play help you manage annoyances, hard times and setbacks.

- Smooth over differences. Using gentle humour often helps you say things that might be otherwise difficult to express in a way that is acceptable and delivers the message effectively.

- Simultaneously relax and energise yourself. Playful communication relieves fatigue and relaxes your body, which allows you to recharge and accomplish more.

- Become more creative. When you loosen up, you free yourself of rigid ways of thinking and being, allowing you to get creative and see things in new ways.

How to develop playful communication

- Try setting aside regular, quality playtime. The more you joke, play and laugh the easier it becomes.

- Find enjoyable activities that loosen you up and help you embrace your playful nature.

- Practice by playing with animals, babies, young children and outgoing people who appreciate playful banter.

SKILL 5: RESOLVE CONFLICT POSITIVELY

Conflict and disagreements are inevitable and unavoidable in relationships. We know that's impossible for two people to have the same needs, opinions, and expectations all the time. Resolving conflict in healthy, constructive ways can strengthen trust between people. When conflict is not perceived as threatening or punishing it fosters freedom, creativity and safety in relationships.

Managing conflicts in a positive, trust-building way is supported by the previous four skills. Once you know how to manage stress, stay emotionally present and aware, communicate non-verbally and use humour and play, you will be better equipped to handle emotionally charged situations and catch and defuse many issues before they escalate.

Tips for resolving conflict in a trust-building way:

- Stay focused in the present. When you are not holding on to old hurts and resentments you can recognise the reality of what's happening now and approach it as a new opportunity for resolving old feelings about conflicts.

- Choose your arguments. Arguments take time and energy, especially if you want to resolve them in a positive way. Consider what is worth arguing about and what is not. Sometimes it makes sense to let it go.

- Forgive. Other people's hurtful behaviour is in the past. To resolve conflict, you need to give up the urge to punish or seek revenge.

- End conflicts that can't be resolved. It takes two people to keep an argument going. You can choose to disengage from a conflict, even if you still disagree.

HOW TO TEACH AND LEARN EI

Now we have a clearer understanding of our human lifecycle development process and a framework to help us understand how our motivations are aligned to our needs.

The question now is how do we do it? How do we put into practice what we know about how people develop emotionally? How can we use it to help us lead more fulfilled lives? In short, how can we give ourselves – and our children – the best of being happy?

'To teach is to learn, to do is to achieve our goals'

In this section we will consider pedagogy as the framework for learning through teaching as part of our EI development. It won't replace education or other traditional learning frameworks but complement them as an additional application that can be used freely to achieve results and learnings.

Pedagogy is the science and art of education, specifically instructional theory. An instructor develops conceptual knowledge and manages the content of learning activities in pedagogical settings. Modern pedagogy has been strongly influenced by the cognitivism of Piaget, 1926, 1936/1975; the social-interactionist theories of Bruner, 1960, 1966, 1971, 1986; and the social and cultural theories of Vygotsky, 1962. These theorists laid a foundation for pedagogy where sequential development of individual mental processes – such as recognising, recalling, analysing, reflecting, applying, creating, understanding, and evaluating - are scaffolded. Students learn as they internalise the procedures, organisation, and structures encountered in social contexts as their own. The learner needs help to integrate prior knowledge with new knowledge. Children must also develop metacognition, or the ability to learn how to learn.

The pedagogue's job is usually distinguished from a teacher's by primarily focusing on teaching children life-preparing knowledge such as social skills and cultural norms. There is also a focus on the care and well-being of the child. Many pedagogical institutions also practice social inclusion. The pedagogue's work also consists of supporting the child in their mental and social development.

INSTRUCTIONAL THEORY

An instructional theory is 'a theory that offers explicit guidance on how to better help people learn and develop.' Instructional theories focus on how to structure material for promoting the education of human beings.

INSTRUCTIONAL THEORY VS LEARNING THEORY

Instructional theory differs from learning theory in that a learning theory describes how learning takes place and an instructional theory prescribes how to better help people learn. Learning theories often inform instructional theory. General theoretical stances for learning theories are behaviourism (learning as response acquisition), cognitivism (learning as knowledge acquisition), humanism (interpersonal and intrapersonal learning), and constructivism (learning as knowledge construction).

TERMS USED IN INSTRUCTIONAL THEORY

Andragogy [an-druh-goh-jee, -goj-ee]. Originally used by Alexander Kapp (a German educator) in 1833, andragogy was developed into a theory of adult education by the American educator Malcolm Knowles. The word comes from the Greek and translates as, 'to lead the man.' Learning strategies focus on mature learning with a mentor that encourages and enables the mature learner by providing access to appropriate resources, and refrains from obtrusive interference.

Diaskagogy [dee-es-kuh-goh-jee, -goj-ee]. A neologism developed for preschool education that focuses on schema building. The caregiver demonstrates factual knowledge, then observes, measures, and modifies behavioural change in a specified direction. The teacher /child relationship in this scenario is one of entertainment. The word for entertainer in Greek translated to Latin is genius. When combined with the Greek 'ago' to 'lead,' the construed meaning is 'to lead the entertainer' and the transliteration from the Greek leads to the word 'diaskagogy', which could be used to describe pre-school education.

Heutagogy [hyoo-tah-goh-jee, -goj-ee]. The term, attributed to Stewart Hase [Southern Cross University] and Chris Kenyon of Australia, is the study of self-determined learning. The word appears to come from an irregular formation of the Greek words heurista meaning to 'discover,' heuretikos meaning 'inventive,' heuriskein meaning to 'find,' and ago to 'lead'; so it is construed to mean 'to lead to invention, discoveries, findings' and consists of learning strategies focused on mature learners where a facilitator enables quested learning to allow for modification of existing knowledge and creation of new knowledge.

Pedagogy [ped-ah-goh-jee, -goj-ee]. The word comes from the Greek pedagogue; in which ped means 'child' and ago means 'lead'; so it literally means 'to lead the child' where a teacher develops conceptual knowledge and manages the content of learning activities.

INSTRUCTIONAL THEORISTS

Socrates (circa 470–399 BC) introduced method of 'elenchus,' where a problem is broken down into a series of questions, the answers to which gradually elicit the sought-after answer. This approach is most strongly felt today in the use of the scientific method, where hypothesis is the first stage of problem solving.

Aristotle (circa 384-322 BC) postulated experience is the source of knowledge and believed that knowledge was gained through experiencing the environment. He believed knowledge was associative, meaning that one idea will trigger the recall of the other, which is a prelude to sequential learning and schema development.

Plato (428/427 BC– 348/347 BC) believed people learn about ideas through reasoning. Plato taught mental discipline. He believed that if we exercised our mind, our mind would strengthen; therefore, he touted rigor and mental discipline.

John Locke (29 August 1632 – 28 October 1704) believed that skills and knowledge are acquired through example and practice, not exhaustive drills that require children to memorise rules or principals; also, that desirable behaviours are learned by unconsciously imitating the manners of role models.

Étienne Bonnot de Condillac's (30 September 1715 – 3 August 1780) doctrine reigned in the schools of France for over fifty years. Condillac's works include *Essays on the origin of human knowledge* (1746), *Treatise on the system* (1749), *Treatise on the senses* (1754), and an extensive course of study in 13 volumes, *Cours d'études* (1767-1773), that emphasise the importance of using the senses to increase learning. Condillac's work is significant to the field of education because he is among the first to emphasise the importance of manipulating matter as well as ideas to construct behavioural learning, advocating a sense-luscious environment to provide a stimulus response-learning environment.

John Dewey (20 October 1859 – 1 June 1952) argued that in order for education to be most effective, content must be presented in a way that allows the student to relate the information to prior experiences, deepening the connection with this new knowledge.

Jean Piaget (9 August 1896 – 17 September 1980) explored changes in internal cognitive structure as well as recognising the contribution of the environment to learning. He identified four stages of mental growth (sensorimotor, preoperational, concrete operational, and formal operational).

B. F. Skinner's (20 March 1904 – 18 August 18, 1990) theories of behaviour were highly influential on many early instructional theorists because their hypotheses can be tested fairly easily with the scientific process.

Benjamin Bloom (21 February 1913 – 13 September 1999), a University of Chicago professor, developed Taxonomy of Education Objectives – one of the first modern codifications of the learning process.

Malcolm S. Knowles (24 August 1913 – 27 November 1997) joined the staff at Boston University in 1959, spending 14 years there, during which time his publications became foundational for adult education discourse in the United States, introducing the instructional theory called andragogy. In 1974 he joined the faculty of North Carolina State University where he developed courses using 'the andragogical model'. He also published a new book on self-directed learning.

Jerome Bruner (born 1 October 1915) explored how mental processes could be linked to teaching (emphasising, among other things, learning through discovery).

Robert M. Gagné (21 August 1916 – 28 April 2002) developed a model that highlighted eight different forms of learning and in 1965 published *Conditions of Learning* for the Florida State University's Department of Educational Research.

Paulo Freire's (19 September 1921 – 2 May 1997) work is significant because of his emphasis on respectful co-operative dialogue involving people working with each other; his concern with praxis, informed action that enhances community and leads us to act in ways that make for justice and human flourishing; his attention to developing consciousness for educating the oppressed; his insistence on situating educational activity in the lived experience of participants; and his ability to transcend the divide between teachers and learners.

EXAMPLE OF EI TEACHING

THE MONTESSORI EDUCATION

A great model of psychosocial and Emotional Intelligence application is the Montessori education system – a system that educates each individual in a rounded and balanced way.

This educational approach was developed by Italian physician and educator Maria Montessori and emphasises independence, freedom within limits, and respect for a child's natural psychological, physical, and social development. Although a range of practices exists under the name 'Montessori', the Association Montessori Internationale (AMI) and the American Montessori Society (AMS) cite these elements as essential:

- Mixed-age classrooms, with classrooms for children aged from two-and-half or three up to six years old.

- Children can choose their activities from a range of options.

- Uninterrupted blocks of work time, ideally three hours.

- A constructivist or 'discovery' model, where children learn concepts from working with materials, rather than by direct instruction.

- Specialised educational materials developed by Montessori and her collaborators.

- Freedom of movement within the classroom.

- A trained Montessori teacher.

Many Montessori schools design their programmes with reference to Montessori's model of human development, and use pedagogy, lessons, and materials introduced in teacher training derived from courses presented by Montessori during her lifetime

HISTORY

Maria Montessori began to develop her philosophy and methods in 1897, attending courses in pedagogy at the University of Rome and reading the educational theory of the previous two hundred years. In 1907, she opened her first classroom, the Casa dei Bambini, or Children's House, in a tenement building in Rome. From the beginning, Montessori based her work on her observations of children and experimentation with the environment, materials, and lessons available to them. She frequently referred to her work as 'scientific pedagogy'. Montessori education spread to the United States in 1911 and became widely known in education and popular publications. However, conflict between Montessori and the American educational establishment, and especially the publication in 1914 of a critical booklet, *The Montessori System Examined* by influential education teacher William Heard Kilpatrick, limited the spread of her ideas, and they languished after 1914. Montessori education returned to the United States in 1960 and has since spread to thousands of schools there. Montessori continued to extend her work during her lifetime, developing a comprehensive model of psychological development from birth to age 24, as well as educational approaches for children ages 0 to three, three to six, and six to 12. She wrote and lectured about ages 12 to 18 and beyond, but these programmes were not developed during her lifetime.

MONTESSORI EDUCATION THEORY

The system is based on self-construction, liberty, and spontaneous activity. Montessori education is fundamentally a model of human development, and an educational approach based on that model. The model has two basic principles. First, children and developing adults engage in psychological self-construction by interacting with their environments. Second, children, especially under the age of six, have an innate path of psychological development. Based on her observations, Montessori believed that children at liberty to choose and act freely within an environment prepared according to her model would act spontaneously for optimal development.

HUMAN TENDENCIES

Montessori saw universal, innate characteristics in human psychology which her son and collaborator Mario Montessori identified as 'human tendencies' in 1957. There is some debate about the exact list, but the following are clearly identified:

- Abstraction
- Activity
- Communication
- Exactness
- Exploration
- Manipulation (of the environment)
- Order
- Orientation
- Repetition
- Self-perfection
- Work (also described as 'purposeful activity')

In the Montessori approach, these human tendencies are seen as driving behaviour in every stage of development, and education should respond to and facilitate their expression.

PREPARED ENVIRONMENT

Montessori's education method called for free activity within a 'prepared environment', meaning an educational environment tailored to basic human characteristics, to the specific characteristics of children at different ages, and to the individual personalities of each child. The function of the environment is to allow the child to develop independence in all areas according to his or her inner psychological directives. In addition to offering access to the Montessori materials appropriate to the age of the children, the environment should exhibit the following characteristics:

- An arrangement that facilitates movement and activity

- Beauty and harmony, and a clean environment

- Construction in proportion to the child and his/her needs

- Limitation of materials, so that only material that supports the child's development is included

- Order.

PLANES OF DEVELOPMENT

Montessori observed four distinct periods, or 'planes', in human development, extending from birth to six years, from six to 12, from 12 to 18, and from 18 to 24. She saw different characteristics, learning modes, and developmental imperatives active in each of these planes, and called for educational approaches specific to each period.

First plane

The first plane extends from birth to around six years of age. During this period, Montessori observed that the child undergoes striking physical and psychological development. The first plane child is seen as an explorer and learner engaged in the developmental work of psychological self-construction and building functional independence. Montessori introduced several concepts to explain this work, including the absorbent mind, sensitive periods, and normalisation.

Absorbent mind: Montessori described the young child's behaviour of effortlessly assimilating the sensorial stimuli of his or her environment, including information from the senses, language, culture, and the development of concepts with the term 'absorbent mind'. She believed that this is a power unique to the first plane, and that it fades as the child approached the age of six.

Sensitive periods: Montessori also observed periods of special sensitivity to particular stimuli during this time which she called the 'sensitive periods'. In Montessori education, the classroom environment responds to these periods by making appropriate materials and activities available while the periods are active in the young child. She identified the following periods and their durations:

- Acquisition of language – from birth to around six years old

- Interest in small objects – from around 18 months to three years old

- Order – from around one to three years old

- Sensory refinement – from birth to around four years old

- Social behaviour – from around two and a half to four years old.

Normalisation: Finally, Montessori observed in children from three to six years old a psychological state she termed 'normalisation'. Normalisation arises from concentration and focus on activity which serves the child's developmental needs, and is characterized by the ability to concentrate as well as 'spontaneous discipline, continuous and happy work, social sentiments of help and sympathy for others.'

Second plane

The second plane of development extends from around six to 12 years old. During this period, Montessori observed physical and psychological changes in children, and developed a classroom environment, lessons, and materials, to respond to these new characteristics. Physically, she observed the loss of baby teeth and the lengthening of the legs and torso at the beginning of the plane, and a period of uniform growth following. Psychologically, she observed the 'herd instinct', or the tendency to work and socialise in groups, as well as the powers of reason and imagination. Developmentally, she believed the work of the second plane child is the formation of intellectual independence, of moral sense, and of social organisation.

Third plane

The third plane of development extends from around 12 to around 18 years of age, encompassing the period of adolescence. Montessori characterised the third plane by the physical changes of puberty and adolescence, but also psychological changes. She emphasised the psychological instability and difficulties in concentration of this age, as well as the creative tendencies and the development of 'a sense of justice and a sense of personal dignity.' She used the term 'valorisation' to describe the adolescents' drive for an externally derived evaluation of their worth. Developmentally, Montessori believed that the work of the third plane child is the construction of the adult self in society.

Fourth plane

The fourth plane of development extends from around 18 to 24 years old. Montessori wrote comparatively little about this period and did not develop an educational program for the age. She envisioned young adults prepared by their experiences in Montessori education at the lower levels ready to fully embrace the study of culture and the sciences in order to influence and lead civilization. She believed that economic independence in the form of work for money was critical for this age, and felt that an arbitrary limit to the number of years in university level study was unnecessary, as the study of culture could go on throughout a person's life.

EDUCATION AND PEACE

As Montessori developed her theory and practice, she came to believe that education had a role to play in the development of world peace. She felt that children allowed to develop according to their inner laws of development would give rise to a more peaceful and enduring civilization. From the 1930s to the end of her life, she gave a number of lectures and addresses on the subject.

THE KANDO EI MODEL

How, and when can we start to begin our Emotional Intelligence self teaching and learning at home? Today! A simple way to start is to use the KANDO Model of EQ.

KANDO EQ education theory model – including programs 1 & 2

- Ethics

- Independence

- Free with limits

- Respect for natural psychological, physical and social development.

HUMAN DEVELOPMENT LIFE CYCLE

- Children and developing adults engage in psychological self-construction through interaction with others and their environments

- Promotion of psychological development.

HUMAN TENDENCIES

The KANDO model covers abstraction, activity, communication, exactness, exploration, manipulation (of the environment), order, orientation, repetition, self-perfection and work (purposeful activity). If you can activate these elements in your children - and yourself you will really feel the difference!

Follow KANDO model and remember that your KANDO coach is there to help you.

ENVIRONMENT

We all live, work and play in our own particular surroundings, and as we have learned from reading about Erikson, Maslow and others, these factors are important. Most of us have little opportunity to change our circumstance and we will certainly be affected by them

For example, if you live in Africa you will only be able to achieve the outputs of your specific cultural and environmental surroundings and won't develop in quite the same way someone from another country.

DEVELOPMENT PHASES

As you read through the following phases, you'll recognise many elements of your own child's development.

PHASE 1: EARLY CHILDHOOD (0 TO 3 YEARS)

- Absorbent mind
- Sensitive periods
- Normalisation.

PHASE 2: MIDDLE TO LATE CHILDHOOD (3 TO 9 YEARS)

- Intellectual independence
- Moral sense
- Social organisation.

PHASE 3: ADOLESCENCE (9 TO 18 YEARS)

- Puberty
- Construction of adult self in society.

PHASE 4: ADULTHOOD (18 YEARS AND UP)

- Embrace culture and sciences
- Influence and leadership
- Economic independence.

KANDO EQ ASSESSMENT

The methods used to Assess / Integrate / Review / Test (AIRT) can be done in different ways to suit you and your circumstances, including family and social knowledge sharing or a 'handing it down' approach.

The KANDO EI programme does not subscribe to a particular fashion in this area – it aims to provide a framework understanding in a simple to understand language as a its platform.

Self assessment Tool 0 - 8 years

This can be done in a number of ways but we suggest that this tool or language is a good model to try.

Take 'The Adult Sampling Domain of Trait Emotional Intelligence' from the table below as the way you'd like your young one to behave when they get older.

According to Erikson, at 18 the individual becomes a young adult, so with this as the timeline 100% is 18 years of age and 0% is just born. Divide it into four equal quarters of development to be considered, give or take a few months change at overlap points. This will help you decide the appropriate language to use with your child at each level, so:

- 0 - 4.5 years (big / core / solid messages – simple wording)

- 4.5 to 9 years (more choices of wording to be used including adult)

- 9 to 13.5 years (adult and more detailed wording)

- 13.5 to 18 years (adult complex wording)

Simply create a question for each emotional state you are seeking to assess, using your own experiences and the way you wish it had been approach.

You might say: 'That Johnny friend of yours seems nice but not very assertive. He seems a bit quiet to me. What do you think?

Remember to dilute the wording and make the whole experience of question and answer enjoyable for your developing child.

Trait Emotional Intelligence & TEIQue
(Psychometric Lab at UCL)

KANDO EQ Assessment Tools are aligned to following the principals of the Trait Emotional Intelligence Research at UCL. We have over 30 years' experience in the field, and also follow Bayesian Theory and evolutionary genetics in this area.

THE ADULT SAMPLING DOMAIN OF TRAIT EMOTIONAL INTELLIGENCE	
Facets	High scorers perceive themselves as...
Adaptability	...flexible and willing to adapt to new conditions.
Assertiveness	...forthright, frank, and willing to stand up for their rights.
Emotion perception (self and others)	...clear about their own and other people's feelings.
Emotion expression	...capable of communicating their feelings to others.
Emotion management (others)	...capable of influencing other people's feelings.
Emotion regulation	...capable of controlling their emotions.
Impulsiveness (low)	...reflective and less likely to give in to their urges.
Relationships	...capable of having fulfilling personal relationships.
Self-esteem	...successful and self-confident.
Self-motivation	...driven and unlikely to give up in the face of adversity.
Social awareness	...accomplished networkers with excellent social skills.
Stress management	...capable of withstanding pressure and regulating stress.
Trait empathy	...capable of taking someone else's perspective.
Trait happiness	...cheerful and satisfied with their lives.
Trait optimism	...confident and likely to 'look on the bright side' of life.

KANDO EI qualified coaches train the trainer programmes

Your qualified coaches provide at-home sessions in a 'train the trainer' form. This means they teach you how to teach your children the value of EI. You can then carry on your teaching practice and ongoing development with peers and with other parents and careers as your circumstances allow.

Our coaches use a pedagogical approach with additional techniques for accelerated learning and for those requiring learning attunement (and for children with learning difficulties).

Sessions cover personal assessment (form/score sheets are available if needed), how to integrate skills/questions/actions using pedagogy, how to review the outcomes using the 'teach me back' approach and questions to test in fun game situations.

KANDO EI games – ages one to 12 years:

- Children learn with EI games

- Children learn with materials and the games

- Children learn through pedagogy.

Range of games

- One to four years (look at me! – teaches emotional self awareness)

- Four to five years (Simon says – teaches flexibility)

- Five to six years (let's dance! – teaches stress tolerance)

- Six to eight years (how others feel – teaches empathy)

- Eight to 10 years (positive thinking – encourages optimism)

- 11 years to 12 years (stand up! – encourages assertiveness).

KANDO EI review

Using the above guide as your benchmark, this is the bit that should be the most fun for you and your child.

Decide which EI outcome you want your child to possess, then teach them it by leading them into play to achieve the emotional intelligence outcome path you want your child to follow.

Remember always to reinforce by asking your child can teach you back and keep repeating with various games until the EI outcome you are concentrating on becomes a habit of behaviour.

KANDO EQ test

As parents we owe it ourselves to support the development of our young ones' emotional intelligence. And while we can guide their choices in life, it's up to them in the end.

Edward De Bono tells us that at the end of the day all decisions are based on emotions, so it's important that – as parents – we help our children get the emotional bit right by teaching, guiding and testing.

A good place to start is to ask your young one to show you how to do the outcome as an actor displaying the emotion desired.

Choosing several participation, competitive sport or group activities to display your youngster's skills is probably a good holistic approach and helps establish the emotional mindset needed to display these behaviours.

When your child is interacting with others, you are not testing just their ability at the activity but, more importantly, focusing on their behaviour with others: are they showing good participation, equality and transparency or fair play?

KANDO EI GAMES

KANDO in Japanese means 'an Inspired state of mind'. In English this means what our mothers taught us as children: 'you can do whatever you put your mind to it'. It means teaching our children to feel their emotions and embrace them.

Try the following games with your children and help them experience and recognise their emotions in a fun way.

LOOK AT ME!

CARER/PARENTS

Make a large cardboard or paper egg and ask your child to decorate it to look like their own face. It's interesting to see how your child seems her or himself.

This activity is designed to teach your child self-awareness and creativity. Encourage your child to decorate their egg to look like her or himself.

You can also use this exercise to teach children how to dress themselves and take care of their hair and face.

Pay close attention to the detail your child puts into their egg. This will help determine their level of self-awareness. You will need to cut a large piece of construction paper into the shape of an egg.

MATERIALS NEEDED:

- Construction paper

- Felt pens

- Yarn

- Scraps of fabric or coloured paper

- Scissors

- Glue

Tell your child this is a chance to show off their talents! Add arms and legs, draw a face with pens, make hair out of yarn, and make clothes for the egg.

SIMON SAYS

This activity is designed to teach your child flexibility.

After you play the game be sure to explain to your child the importance of being able to be flexible in certain situations, especially when playing with others, when plans change, etc.

Stand up and see if you can follow these simple commands. Remember, you only do the things that Simon Says! If a command does not start with the words 'Simon says' the child should not do it.

- Simon Says put your hand on your head

- Simon Says jump up high

- Stoop down low

- Simon Says open your mouth

- Close your eyes

- Simon Says touch your nose

- Simon Says wave your arms in the air

- Touch your toes

- Simon Says put your right hand under your chin

- Simon Says jump up and down on one foot

- Turn all the way around

- Simon Says take two steps forward

- Simon Says take three steps backwards

- Simon Says game over

- Simon Says hug your carer/friends/parents.

LET'S DANCE!

This activity is designed to help your child deal with stress. If your child can learn techniques to deal with stress at this young age, it should help them manage it better as they grow up. Encourage your child to relieve their stress in a productive manner.

Ask your child the following questions. Do you they angry? Have you ever been sent to your room because you got in trouble? How do you deal with it when things don't go your way? One way to deal with it is to dance!

Put on your favourite music and dance.

Talk <u>about</u> other things the child can do if they feel angry or frustrated.

HOW OTHERS FEEL

Understanding how others feel helps us get along with other people. Before doing something to someone else, we should think about how it would make us feel if someone did the same thing to us.

Working with the child, circle YES or NO for each question below.

WOULD YOU LIKE IT IF SOMEONE...

Teased you?	YES	NO
Called you a name?	YES	NO
Pushed you out of a queue at school?	YES	NO
Broke your favourite toy?	YES	NO
Laughed when you made a mistake?	YES	NO
Blamed you for something you didn't do?	YES	NO
Took your share of something?	YES	NO

Discuss the answers with child and take the opportunity to talk about how other people would feel in those situations.

POSITIVE THINKING

Talk to your child about aspects of themselves they wish they could change. Explain that some of those things can be changed and some can't, and they don't have to feel unhappy about the things you can't change. Remember, negative feelings are caused by negative thoughts. The easiest way to stop feeling miserable is to change thoughts about the thing that is bothering you. Instead of feeling bad or embarrassed, choose one of two things.

- Change the things about yourself that bother you.

- Change your thoughts about yourself you don't like.

What could you do in each of these situations? Discuss what you could do to change your feelings to positive ones.

- You like the colour of your best friend's hair and wish yours was the same colour.

- You are sensitive about your weight (too fat or too thin).

- You are short and think that people pick on short people.

- You think you are not good at sports because you're always the last one chosen for teams.

- You think your nose is too big.

- You are shy and would like to make friends more easily, but you have trouble going up to other kids and starting a conversation.

Talk about the answers and anything else that comes up in the conversation; your child will have her or his own preoccupations and insecurities. Talk about turning negatives into positives and practical ways of dealing with situations.

STAND UP FOR YOURSELF!

Being assertive doesn't mean being mean or bossy: it really is okay to let people know what you want and what you like or dislike.

Ask your child to look at each situation below and discuss how the character could have been more assertive.

THE SATISFACTION DILEMMA

Jimmy's dad has always wanted him to be a football star. Jimmy didn't want to play football; he preferred to be in the school band. But he did not want to let his dad down. Jimmy wanted to please his dad so he played football instead of joining the band.

THE INTERRUPTION

Every time you make a phone call to your best friend, your older brother interrupts your conversation and tells you to hang up the phone. You do not want to make him angry.

PEER PRESSURE

Jason, Elizabeth and Chad are your best friends. They have decided to skip an English class because they did not finish the homework assignment. You do not want to miss the lesson class but you don't want to annoy your friends.

KANDO EI & REPETITIVE LEARNING:

KANDO considers some aspects of learning as tools and provides discussion elements that can be adopted for use with all children. We recognise that some learners have particular ways of learning that are suited to their individual choice and as such we recommend a degree of flexibility in the way Emotional Intelligence is taught.

OUTCOMES ARE EVERYTHING

We believe that by using the KANDO method, repeating and working with your child, you can make a huge difference to their emotional development.

As with so many things in life, you get out what you put in. Working with your child now will reap real rewards as they grow and develop. As you look at the mature, well-rounded and emotionally intelligent young person you have raised, you should be proud of yourself.

See you in the next book....

12508977R00066

Printed in Great Britain
by Amazon.co.uk, Ltd.,
Marston Gate.